*it first-hand working at Goodyear. The book is well written and easy to understand.*

**Jean-Claude Kihn,** *Former CTO and President of the*
*Europe/Middle East business,*
*Goodyear Tire & Rubber Company*

*Jim Euchner's book ushers in the innovation enterprise. As we emerge from the unchartered waters of a post-pandemic world, A CEO's greatest driver will categorically be innovation. Lean Startup presents a practical model to harness chaos into competitive advantage. My experience personally interviewing over 1,000 top CEOs leads me to believe that* Lean Startup in Large Organizations *could arguably be the most important book an enterprise CEO reads in 2022.*

**Robert Reiss,** *Founder and CEO, The CEO Forum Group*

*"The companies that squander innovative opportunities are often the same corporations searching for new avenues of growth because prospects in their core have stalled." Jim is one of a few rare individuals who have a firm foot hold in both theory and practice. This helps to ensure that* Lean Startup in Large Organizations *is well grounded, relevant, and delivers impact as it provides readers with a set of practical tools to help bring a concept from idea to validated business.*

**Tim Baines,** *Professor, Aston Business School*

# Lean Startup in Large Organizations

# Lean Startup in Large Organizations

## Overcoming Resistance to Innovation

James A. Euchner

Routledge
Taylor & Francis Group
A PRODUCTIVITY PRESS BOOK

Cover design: Greg Euchner

First published 2022
by Routledge
605 Third Avenue, New York, NY 10158

and by Routledge
2 Park Square, Milton Park, Abingdon, Oxon, OX14 4RN

*Routledge is an imprint of the Taylor & Francis Group, an informa business*

ISBN: 978-1-032-20026-2 (hbk)
ISBN: 978-1-138-35913-0 (pbk)
ISBN: 978-0-429-43388-7 (ebk)

DOI: 10.4324/9780429433887

Typeset in Minion
by Deanta Global Publishing Services, Chennai, India

*To Nancy, whose love and support made my career and*

*this book possible. I will love you always and forever.*

# Contents

# Preface: Why This Book

I was inspired to write this book by a desire to help companies avoid missed opportunities. My goal is to help readers move more quickly and surely through the difficult territory of corporate innovation—one that requires navigating the world of pure innovation with the world of corporate norms, advantages, and constraints.

Innovation often languishes within established corporations because they are unable to manage the relationship between the new venture and the ongoing business. Ironically, the companies that squander innovative opportunities are often the same corporations searching for new avenues of growth because prospects in their core have stalled. In fact, history is replete with disruption of incumbent companies by innovations that the companies themselves had pioneered but could not get out of the labs; they snatched defeat from the jaws of victory because organizational issues got in the way of innovation.

The Lean Startup is a set of practices that help to bring a concept from idea to validated business. It can help incumbents to respond more effectively to digital disruption, to create more innovative cultures, and to increase the speed and reliability of their innovation efforts. But Lean Startup methods require adaptation to be effective in the context of a large corporation. This book focuses on those adaptations and why they are necessary. It builds on my experience launching businesses at Goodyear Tire & Rubber Company and at Pitney Bowes Corporation and on the theories of some of the leading thinkers in innovation management.

I have learned from these thought leaders directly and indirectly, through studying their theories and trying to apply them, as individual practice and as a synthesized system. I started by reading their books and attempting to apply their findings in ongoing innovation projects. As Editor in Chief of *Research-Technology Management*, I also had the opportunity to interview them about their work. Those interviews were an opportunity to dig deeply into the practical challenges I confronted in applying their theories in the real world, and they pushed beyond the theory to the nitty-gritty issues that emerge in the messy work of corporate innovation. I can attest that the theories work in practice, but there is a substantial learning curve.

This book discusses both Lean Startup and a set of organizational practices that make it work in the corporate context. While the Lean Startup practices accelerate learning, the complementary practices help overcome organizational resistance. The additional practices—which are described in this book—help both to manage internal frictions and to enable an internal startup to leverage the assets of the core business.

The practices described in this book are "Yes … AND" practices: They complement the core principles of the Lean Startup itself. They have been tested—and have led to success—in real-world corporate settings. Although no two corporate cultures are exactly the same, many of the challenges are frighteningly common. These practices are a starting point for beginning the journey.

# Acknowledgments

I would like to acknowledge my colleagues and friends at NYNEX (now Verizon), Pitney Bowes, and Goodyear Tire & Rubber Company, who shaped my thinking about the practice of innovation. We were constantly experimenting with how to make our initiatives both profitable and user-centered—and how to make them work in corporate settings. We learned enough to create a lot of value, but we also stubbed our toes quite a bit. I think that when we failed, we usually learned from our failures. Abhijit Ganguly and Erin Spring, in particular, helped to test the ideas in this book in practice.

I would also like to thank the thought leaders I interviewed for *Research-Technology Management* over the past ten years. I learned a lot from them, experimented with their theories in practice, and pushed them in the interviews to discuss how their theories work in corporate settings. Excerpts of eight of these interviews are included in this book, including interviews with Steve Blank, Eric Ries, Gina O'Connor, John Rossman, Adrian Slywotzky, Ron Adner, Vijay Govindarajan, and Michael Tushman. I thank all of them for their insights and for the time that they spent with me. I owe a lot to their research. I would also like to thank the Innovation Research Interchange, which publishes the journal, and Ed Bernstein, its president, for his support.

I have been fortunate to have had several mentors during my career, and I would like to thank them. They taught me more than I can acknowledge, especially Tim Baines, Michael Critelli, Jean-Claude Kihn, Ed Thomas, John Thomas, and Eric von Hippel.

MaryAnne Hamilton edited most of the writing included in this book. She made everything I wrote better for over ten years. Jill Lawrence and Andrea Kates encouraged me to continue writing the book, even when I was ready to give up.

I would also like to thank my children, Gregory, Richard, and Marshall, for their love and support. They taught me both joy and that each new venture is its own adventure. I give thanks always for Christ, who sustains me.

# About the Author

 **Jim Euchner** is a customer-centered technology executive with more than 25 years of experience leading innovation, strategy, advanced IT, and R&D in Fortune 500 companies. He has a track record of delivering top-line and bottom-line growth through radical process innovation, new product introduction, and the launch of new businesses. His experience includes senior leadership positions in the automotive, manufacturing, telecommunications, and oil and gas industries.

Most recently, Jim was Vice President of Global Innovation at Goodyear Tire & Rubber Company, where he led the development of new businesses and incubated and launched four businesses on three continents. Prior to his work at Goodyear, Jim held positions as Vice President of Growth Strategy and Innovation at Pitney Bowes, Inc. and as Vice President, Network Systems Advanced Technology at Bell Atlantic (now Verizon).

Jim is an established expert in driving growth inside large enterprises. He was a pioneer in the use of anthropology and design methods inside companies and has developed effective practices for the use of Lean Startup techniques in the corporate context. Throughout his career, Jim has focused on the practical use of emerging technologies, including expert systems, machine learning, cloud-based predictive analytics, operations research, and the Internet of Things. He has published over 100 papers, interviews, and columns. Two of his papers were included in *Innovative Applications of Artificial Intelligence*, and one was a finalist for the prestigious Edelman Award for achievement in operations research. He holds 13 U.S. patents, including 1 that combines neural network technology with knowledge-based approaches to character recognition.

Jim is Editor in Chief of *Research-Technology Management*, a peer-reviewed journal for practitioners of innovation, technology, and research management. He is also Visiting Professor at Aston Business School (UK), where he is helping manufacturing firms move from product-centric to services-led business models. Jim is particularly interested in business model innovation and the effective use of Lean Startup approaches in large organizations.

Jim is industry Co-Chair of the Aston University Advanced Services Partnership and was a member of the Scientific Advisory Council for the Nissan autonomous vehicle program. He is also Co-Founder of the MIT Innovation Laboratory, a consortium to nurture innovation in organizations. Jim has published and spoken extensively on innovation and technology management.

Jim received his Bachelor of Science degree from Cornell University in mechanical and aerospace engineering and his Master of Science degree from Princeton University, where he was a Guggenheim Fellow. He also holds an MBA from Southern Methodist University.

# 1

## *Introduction*

Lean Startup is a collection of practices for creating a new business from scratch. The practices are designed to deal with the conditions of extreme uncertainty that come with starting any new business [Ries, 2011]. Lean Startup is designed to surface critical assumptions and then to test each one with rapid experiments. Thousands of startups have used the Lean Startup methodology to move more quickly and more surely toward a viable business [Blank, 2018].

Lean Startup has also attracted many adherents in large enterprises. Some companies, like GE, have made it part of their operating system; at GE, Lean Startup has been implemented in a way analogous to the way Six Sigma was implemented, as a widely taught system of practices [Goldstein and Euchner, 2017]. Other companies have adopted Lean Startup only in separate new-venture incubators, isolated from the core business, where the method can be practiced in its purest form. Still others have adopted parts of the system, integrating them into their current way of doing innovation [Koen, Golm and Euchner, 2014]. But Lean Startup has not been as successful in large companies as it has been in startups [Blank, 2021].

Understanding the challenges Lean Startup presents for large organizations and beginning to address them is the object of this book. The essays, interviews, and articles included in this collection offer insight into both Lean Startup and the challenges it faces when implemented in large organizations.

Lean Startup practices are all about learning: Learning about the customer, learning about the limits of technology, learning about the different elements of the business model. Unfortunately, the very practices that make this learning possible can be threatening to existing organizations. The practices by their very nature create a set of fears and reactions that

DOI: 10.4324/9780429433887-1

must be managed for Lean Startup to succeed. This book names the fears and resistances and discusses a set of practices that addresses them. The complementary practices are based on both theories of researchers and their application in practice [Euchner and Ganguly, 2014].

The book begins by summarizing the Lean Startup approach. In Chapter 2, "Lean Startup in a Nutshell," I provide an overview of the methodology, along with excerpts of interviews with Eric Ries and Steve Blank, the principal creators of Lean Startup. The core of Lean Startup is seven principles that, taken together, make the overall system work. Three of these principles relate to *how* to learn using iterative experimentation: The Lean Learning Loop, the Minimum Viable Product (MVP), and the pivot-or-persist decision. The next three principles relate to *what* to learn, conceptualized as three core hypotheses that must be validated to create a successful business: The Value Hypothesis, the Business Model Hypothesis, and the Growth Hypothesis. The final principle is innovation accounting.

Making Lean Startup work in the context of a large company brings unique challenges. The very practices that lead to success in finding a product-market fit can create problems for creating a venture-corporation fit. For each Lean Startup practice, there is a threat to the existing corporation that must be managed. The threat—which is real—leads to a fear, which operates at an emotional (and often unspoken) level. An overview of the threats, the fears that they induce, and a set of complementary practices that alleviate the fears are the subjects of Chapter 3, "What's Different in Large Organizations."

The first fear is *a fear of chaos*. Lean Startup is a very dynamic process, based on a rapid sequence of experiments and pivots. This can seem very chaotic inside established companies, which generally have well-established new product development practices. Meshing the somewhat chaotic practices of Lean Startup with the expectations for discipline and metrics most companies bring to new product development is a threshold issue for the adoption of Lean Startup. Chapter 4, titled "Containing the Chaos," discusses the Innovation Stage-Gate, a mechanism for doing so. It includes excerpts from an interview with Gina O'Connor, who has studied innovation structures that work in corporate settings and how to staff them.

Chapter 5 addresses *the fear of distraction*. Lean Startup practices can interfere with the combination of core competencies and processes the company relies on to provide discipline and generate profit *in its current business* [Govindarajan and Trimble, 2010]. These well-established ways of operating create efficiencies, but they conflict with the needs of a new venture. Executives quite naturally worry about disruption to their operations, while people in functional roles worry about the risk to their careers of operating outside of their core mandates. Chapter 5, "Working with the Performance Engine," discusses several methods for constructively managing conflict between the innovation team and the corporate functions. It includes an excerpt from an article that Abhijit Ganguly and I wrote on business experiments that addresses the conflict with corporate functions that arises in doing this type of work.

New ventures within corporations must not only create a compelling new business; they must create one that aligns with corporate strategy as well. Often, however, growth strategies are not clearly stated, and the innovation team is left to discover unstated boundaries. Lean Startup, with its focus on exploration and pivots, can create *a fear that the company will drift too far from its core*. Alas, misalignments are often discovered too late in the process to be corrected, to the disappointment of both executives and innovation teams—and to the detriment of both the hosting company and the new venture. Chapter 6 discusses "Achieving Strategic Alignment," with a focus on the importance of finding opportunities that build on the assets of the mother ship. The core practice is the identification of "asset-based opportunity spaces." Amazon is a master of leveraging assets to move into great new businesses, and this chapter includes extracts from an interview with John Rossman, who created the Marketplaces business at Amazon. The interview illustrates asset-based innovation from the perspective of a master practitioner.

In large organizations, the dominant business model is well established and often sacrosanct. But a new venture may need to go to market with a different business model if it is to succeed. This requires overcoming the inertia of the dominant model and *the fear of cannibalization*—the fear that the new business will succeed by feeding on customers and revenue streams of the core business. The first step in addressing this fear is simply to consider a full range of alternatives and to assess not only their profitability but their impact on the core business. Chapter 7, "Introducing a New Business Model," discusses a process for managing risks to the core business called the Business Model Pyramid. Two key concepts in managing these risks are business model archetypes and innovation ecosystems. This chapter includes excerpts from interviews with Adrian

Slywotzky, who codified business model archetypes, and Ron Adner, who systematized analysis of the risks of operating in an ecosystem that you do not control.

A new venture inside an established company is always at risk because it competes with the core for valuable resources. The *fear of resource bleed* from the core business can smother the new venture. To succeed, the new company needs to be placed organizationally in a way that enables it to leverage assets of the core business without being smothered by it. Chapter 8, "Organizing for Growth," discusses the Separate-but-Connected model, first proposed by Vijay Govindarajan and Chris Trimble, and the range of practical issues one confronts in implementing it. Vijay Govindarajan provides additional [Govindarajan and Trimble, 2010] insight in excerpts from an interview with him that is included in the chapter.

Chapter 9 discusses "Making the Bet to Win." A new venture that has been demonstrated to be profitable can still fail if the parent company does not invest in its growth. In order to make such investments, executives need to learn along with the venture; if they do not, they are unlikely to overcome the bias that results from a preference for the known over the unknown. The *fear of the unknown* will dominate, dressed in prudence. Making good financial investments in radically new businesses requires first an investment of time for learning—learning about the domain, the customers, and how they want to do business. It also requires developing the flexibility of mind that enables leaders to both exploit the

**TABLE 1.1**

Organization of the Book

| Core Dilemma | Goal | Complementary Practice | Thought Leaders |
|---|---|---|---|
| Fear of chaos | Containing the chaos | An Innovation Stage-Gate | Gina O'Connor |
| Fear of distraction | Working with the performance engine | Graduated Engagement | Abhijit Ganguly and Jim Euchner |
| Loss of identity | Achieving strategic alignment | Asset-based opportunity spaces | John Rossman |
| Fear of cannibalization | Introducing a new business model | The Business Model Pyramid | Adrian Slywotzky Ron Adner |
| Fear of resource bleed | Organizing for growth | The Separate-but-Connected model for incubation | Vijay Govindarajan |
| Fear of the unknown | Making the bet to win | Ambidextrous leadership | Michael Tushman |

core and innovate. Michael Tushman calls this capability "ambidextrous leadership." Excerpts of an interview with Tushman are included in the chapter.

The book concludes with a summary of practices titled, "Yes ... And: Making Lean Startup Work in Large Organizations." Lean Startup practices are powerful—I might go so far as to say essential—to new business innovation. But these practices are not enough to enable internal ventures to thrive. The final chapter summarizes Lean Startup, the organizational reactions it induces, and the practices proposed for addressing them (see Table 1.1).

# 2

## *Lean Startup in a Nutshell: What Every Executive Should Know about Lean Startup*

Lean Startup is a collection of practices for creating a new business from scratch. The practices are designed to deal with what one of the creators of Lean Startup, Eric Ries, refers to as "conditions of extreme uncertainty" [Ries, 2011, 2017]. They focus on progressively reducing uncertainty by surfacing the basic assumptions that must be true for the business to succeed and testing each one with rapid experiments.

Lean Startup began in the startup community in Silicon Valley. Since its beginnings in the early 2000s, thousands of startups have used the Lean Startup process to move more quickly and surely toward a viable business [Blank, 2018]. Steve Blank provided a summary of the experience of 1500 teams sponsored by the National Science Foundation in a blog posting titled, "Making a Dent in the Universe – Results from the NSF I-Corps" [Blank, 2012]. The goal of the NSF I-Corps was very focused: "to teach researchers how to move their technology from an academic lab into the commercial world." The program was assessed based on the reporting of the participants at the end of the program (which was focused on the front-end of the process—defining a Minimum Viable Product and refining a business model). By the end of the class, over 95% believed that they had found a scalable business model, and 98% felt that they had found a "product/market fit."

Lean Startup has also attracted many adherents in large enterprises. Some companies, like GE, have made it part of their operating system; at GE, Lean Startup is taught in a way analogous to the way Six Sigma has been taught, as a coherent system of practices that can be used by

DOI: 10.4324/9780429433887-2

teams to address their innovation issues [Goldstein and Euchner, 2017]. Other companies have adopted Lean Startup only in separate new-venture incubators, isolated from the core business, where it can be practiced in its purest form. Still others have adopted parts of the system, integrating them into their current way of doing innovation [Koen, Golm and Euchner, 2014]. Lean Startup has not been as successful in these large companies as it has in startups, however [Blank, 2021].

Understanding the challenges that Lean Startup presents for large organizations, and beginning to address them, is the object of this book. Doing so requires a basic understanding of its key principles and its guiding philosophy. The underlying philosophy of Lean Startup is a focus on reducing uncertainty—and hence risk—through rapid, iterative, continual learning. This philosophy is enacted in seven principles that guide businesses in *how to learn, what to learn, and how to keep track of learning and results.*

This chapter provides an executive overview of Lean Startup. It includes excerpts of interviews with Eric Ries and Steve Blank, the founders of the method. A particular focus of these interviews is the challenge of adopting Lean Startup in corporate settings [Ries and Euchner, 2013; Blank and Euchner, 2018].

## THE GENESIS AND FUTURE OF LEAN STARTUP

### AN INTERVIEW WITH STEVE BLANK

We have 100 years of tools and techniques, mostly out of business schools, about the execution of business models; even as late as the turn of the century, however, we had no explicit tools for managing innovation or searching for the right business model for a venture ...

The first insight I had was that, unlike companies that are executing a plan—that is, dealing with difficult issues but known issues—startups are dealing mostly with unknowns: unknown customer, unknown channel, unknown pricing, even an unknown feature set that customers actually care about. Once you understand that you are dealing with a lot of unknowns in your business plan, you realize that you have a series of untested hypotheses. That's a big idea.

What naturally followed from that is that we had no methodology to validate or invalidate those hypotheses. Customer development was the first piece of the puzzle: getting out of the building and trying to validate some of your assumptions about customers and their needs. This is summarized in one of the mantras of the Lean idea: There are no facts inside the building, so get the hell out of the building.

Eric [Ries] added an important element to the approach, which was Agile product development, which I wasn't familiar with at the time … Agile Engineering … is building the product incrementally and iteratively; you build the product a piece at a time and constantly get feedback about whether those are right things for the customer. It turns out that Agile Engineering … is a perfect match for customer development … [Together] they were used to develop these things we called minimum viable products, or MVPs. An MVP is what we use with customers outside the building, or with partners or regulators, to get us the most learning at any point in time. The MVP is used to validate or invalidate assumptions. This notion of an MVP was a big idea.

The third piece of the puzzle was the Business Model Canvas. As I taught more and more of this stuff, I realized that there was a need to map and keep track of all the hypotheses that you were testing. The Business Model Canvas, which was developed by Alexander Osterwalder and his collaborators, was a great tool for this. What Osterwalder did was to make a single diagram that captured the nine most important things that an entrepreneur needs to worry about on day one. It was kind of a shorthand for entrepreneurs to think about what they should be testing to create their businesses … The canvas causes you to ask the right questions …

Stanford [University] gave me the opportunity to put all of these pieces together into a new curriculum … I wrote a new class putting together all the pieces that I'd learned about Lean and all the pieces I'd seen about teamwork and how startups actually get built … The class had the following format: Every week, we would teach the students some part about a business model. What's a customer? What's a channel? How do you think about pricing? How do you keep and grow customers? How do you run experiments for this stuff? How do you measure success? … And then, the students had to get out of the classroom, speak to 10 to 15 customers, and build the minimum viable product. This happened every week.

[The whole thing got a big boost when the Head of Commercialization at the National Science Foundation called and said,] "We think you've invented the scientific method for entrepreneurship" … Six and a half years later, we've put over 1,500 teams of the country's best scientists through the program …

[Most] large corporations have awakened to the observation that … the 21st century's a pretty different environment than the 20th century was … [For] the first time ever, startups, which used to be considered ankle-biters, are now not just competitors, but rapacious competitors who are operating in ways you're not allowed to operate, often at the edges of regulations … [S]tartups now have more capital than you do, [too]. That's an amazing, mind-blowing fact.

Large companies aren't stupid. They're looking at what startups are doing and trying to adopt startup tools and techniques, trying to run incubators and accelerators, sponsoring hackathons and maker spaces, and so on.

But here's the conclusion: almost all of those have failed. They did not translate into top-line or bottom-line growth for the company … What happened? We created a series of disconnected activities, confusing that with a process. There's nothing wrong with an incubator, there's nothing wrong with an internal I-Core program, but they're not wired to deliver an end-to-end solution that gets over the finish line. The finish line is bringing the new business to scale, and most companies just haven't figured out how to do that yet.

[Remember], if you're a venture capitalist, you have 10 or 15 things in your portfolio. One or two will pay back at least half the fund, but of the other 10, some will be completely dead, some in the land of the living dead, and some will be singles. And don't forget that, as they build their portfolio, VCs have an innovation funnel that sees hundreds if not thousands of deals to get to the 10 to 15 that they invest it. Most companies don't understand that, if they want to build internally, they need the equivalent of that funnel. It's not just about running experiments to get one out well, but looking at hundreds of things, including external startups, new technologies, maybe internal ideas. If you don't have that scale, then maybe you ought to be buying things rather than trying to build them internally …

I think we're watching the creative destruction of the Fortune 1000, in part because of activist investors forcing a short-term focus on their leadership. It might be that a new configuration will emerge that defines where innovation happens. It might be that what you see are companies buying innovation rather than building it.

## WHAT LARGE COMPANIES CAN LEARN FROM STARTUPS

### AN INTERVIEW WITH ERIC RIES

The biggest insight that I've had as an entrepreneur, working at many companies of very different sizes, is that the defining characteristic of a startup is its environment of extreme uncertainty. We often don't even really know who the customer is. In traditional lean thinking, you look at everything through the eyes of the customer. You examine your supply chain, your manufacturing process, your inventory and ask, "Does the customer care about that?" And if the customer doesn't care, then it's a form of waste.

But whose eyes do we evaluate our systems and processes through if we don't know who the customer is in the first place? That really is the crux of the lean startup question: Can we develop a set of techniques akin to lean manufacturing that are appropriate to a startup? Can we apply the concepts of lean thinking—faster cycle time, reduction in lot size, bringing customers into the process early—not just to build a product efficiently but to discover efficiently what the right product to build is ….

The core idea is that every new business rests on a series of hypotheses—we use the word hypothesis to remind ourselves that building a business is actually a scientific enterprise, or it can be—and we conduct experiments to find out whether we are really on the path to a sustainable business …

Facebook is a good example of a business that had addressed the critical risks of its business. Even if they didn't yet have any gross numbers to brag about, they were able to demonstrate that they had a business. They had addressed both the value hypothesis and the growth hypothesis.

For the value hypothesis, the question is, "Do customers find the product valuable?" You need to have more than a good story or a few anecdotes, but evidence that customers find the product valuable. In Facebook's case, even though they didn't have very many customers yet, of the customers they did have, 50% would use the product every day. So, it was a highly addictive, highly engaging experience for the customers that did use it. They had really good evidence that customers found it valuable. Users were willing to trade a scarce resource—namely, their time and attention—in order to get the benefits of the product.

The second question is, "Given that we've got one customer who finds our product valuable, how are we going to get more?" We call this the growth hypothesis. In the case of Facebook, because of the viral nature of the product, when they moved onto a new college campus, they would go from zero market share to basically 100% of the campus using their product in something like two weeks.

Even though the gross numbers were really small—we call this a micro-scale experiment—even though the scale of it was quite small, the evidence was strong that they were onto something; they had the seeds of a sustainable business …

The companies that I've seen be successful with this create real startups inside the company. It's an organizational structure that works. We call these internal startups semi-autonomous teams. They are cross-functional teams with people who are dedicated full time to the startup. They have bonus and accountability targets that are denominated in innovation accounting not the general accounting of the main company. And they're given what I call a "sandbox for innovation": a set of rules to operate by for innovation.

I'll give you an example from one of my clients. Their innovation team was allowed to affect no more than 1% of the total number of customers the company had. That was the sandbox. So, if the company had 100,000 customers, the internal startup could mess with a thousand of them, but only a thousand. And within the sandbox, they could do whatever they wanted. Even if the startup completely screwed up, they would have cost the firm at most 1% of its customers. That's such a small number, that the company could not only afford the hit to the bottom line but could also afford to make it right to any customers that were adversely affected ...

It says, "If we follow the rules, you will give us the freedom to do whatever we need to do within those boundaries. And we will handle any issues that we create." The teams that work that way I've seen be incredibly effective ...

The scheme that I think is the best for companies that want to be the most avant-garde is to say, look, our default assumption is that a new startup is going to become a new division. If one of the existing divisions wants it to become part of its division, they have to buy it back from corporate just as they would in an M&A process ...

But the thing that never works is for the startup to have to go to a foreign department and ask for something as a favor. That's tough ...

Unfortunately, a lot of the companies that I have seen have no accountability built into their innovation functions, at all. The lean startup approach is all about driving accountability but doing so using the metrics that matter for a startup business.

We are still at the cutting edge with this stuff within corporations. We are just learning about the right way to make startups work in that context, but I'm very excited about the possibilities.

## THE FIRST THREE PRINCIPLES: HOW TO LEARN

The first three principles of Lean Startup focus on *how to learn*. There are three Lean Startup practices that enable this learning: Lean Learning Loops, the Minimum Viable Product, and the pivot-or-persist decision.

### Lean Learning Loops

Experimentation is at the heart of the Lean Startup approach. Lean Startup practitioners design and execute *business* experiments in the same way that laboratory scientists design *scientific* experiments—by framing hypotheses and creating experiments to test them. The Lean Learning Loop (LLL) is the name Lean Startup uses for a cycle of experimentation.

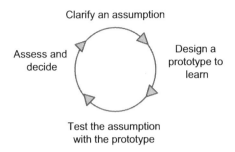

Clarify an assumption

Assess and decide

Design a prototype to learn

Test the assumption with the prototype

**FIGURE 2.1**
Lean Learning Loops

Lean Learning Loops make up the basic construct of the Lean Startup method (see Figure 2.1).

In a single Lean Learning Loop, an innovation team:

1. Frames a hypothesis
2. Designs an experiment to test the hypothesis
3. Conducts the experiment, and then
4. Reviews the results to asses whether they confirm or disconfirm the hypothesis and decide on the next steps.

A Lean Learning Loop can be conducted to learn about almost anything important to the business—the attractiveness of particular features of a product, an estimation of the value created, or the most efficient price point. An experiment can also be designed to test the viability of a channel or the attractiveness of a customer segment; it can be used to understand the costs of delivering a solution or the potential issues that might arise in working with a partner. As each loop delivers new information, the team can zero in on the product design and the business model. In short, Lean Learning Loops are the building blocks of the Lean Startup method.

A team I led at Goodyear, for example, designed an experiment to test the viability of a concept for a "green tire"—one that included significantly more recycled material than a typical tire. The concept would be costly to deliver, but it addressed a known desire among an important customer segment. The question the team wanted to answer was whether people would pay enough to make the concept viable. An experiment was designed to answer this question.

The hypothesis was that customers who were concerned about the environment would pay more for an eco-friendly tire. To test this hypothesis, we selected two Goodyear tire stores in California as test locations. These locations were selected because of their demographics; if the test was not positive there, the team reasoned, it would not be positive anywhere.

The tires did not yet exist (though we had conceived of a means of delivering them), so we created prototypes—new tires with a "New Earth" logo engraved on them. We developed displays and marketing materials for the tires and set them up in the selected stores. Team members manned the stores, and we monitored traffic and customer response over a two-week period. When a customer decided to buy the tires, we informed them that they were part of a research experiment and offered them a discount coupon for their tire purchase.

The experiment disproved our hypothesis. Some customers found the concept attractive, but they would not accept any compromise in tire performance or pay any premium for such a tire. In fact, the customers expected a discount on the tires. This information was a key factor in the decision to discontinue the project. The experiment was a success because it saved significant R&D investment and redirected the innovation team to another concept.

In another example, Pitney Bowes used a business experiment to test the channel for a new postage metering solution. The new concept was novel and addressed a new segment for Pitney Bowes: Very small businesses and individuals who were currently using stamps. The concept we proposed included the ability for customers to customize the images on the stamps the meter printed.

The team hypothesized that the meter could be sold to customers through the company's telemarketing operation. We set up an experiment in which agents were taught to "drop down" to the new offering if the customer decided not to purchase the company's traditional meter. Customers were directed to a web page that showed the meter and its features, although the meter did not yet exist. We measured the rate at which customers placed an order for the concept at different price points for both inbound and outbound telemarketing. The results were very promising. They enabled the innovation team to create a fact-based business case that led to a significant investment in product development.

A Lean Learning Loop is generally a quick, relatively inexpensive, targeted endeavor designed to yield answers to a specific question quickly. Designing a successful learning loop can take some skill. One useful approach is to consider several alternative designs and have others on the team challenge them. The challenges usually center on what can be done to create a "good enough" simulation faster or more inexpensively. More detail on the design of business experiments can be found in "Conducting Business Experiments," by Ganguly and Euchner, excerpts of which are included in Chapter 4.

## Minimum Viable Product

A business experiment generally requires some form of a prototype (see Figure 2.2). Teams must have something—whether it is a web page describing features or a mocked-up tire—to show customers and test hypotheses. The Lean Startup method, which emerged in the software industry, coined the term Minimum Viable Product to describe the prototype used for testing. An MVP is a product that has a very limited (minimal) scope but is useful to and usable by (viable for) some set of customers. The MVP is designed to prove that the product concept is attractive to at least some customers and can succeed in the market.

As Lean Startup has been applied to physical products, innovation teams have borrowed other types of prototypes from the world of design, which has developed a more diverse set of practices for developing and testing prototypes prior to market entry. Many of these kinds of prototypes are created to test a concept or feature before a product is marketed. Thus, in the physical product world, prototypes may include:

- *Probes*—Low-fidelity, nonfunctioning prototypes, such as storyboards or foam-core models, designed to provoke a response to an idea; the idea of a probe is to validate or invalidate the existence of a hypothesized need

**FIGURE 2.2**
The Minimum Viable Product

- *Technical prototypes*—Prototypes designed to demonstrate specific functional capabilities
- *Concept prototypes*—Nonfunctioning or "Wizard of Oz" prototypes designed to assess whether the proposed solution would work in the customer's world
- *Business prototypes*—Small-scale tests of an element of the business model designed to assess and understand how to manage a particular element of risk in the business model
- *Minimum Viable Products*—Prototypes that provide the minimum functionality that is usable by a set of customers.

Most of these prototypes are, strictly speaking, not MVPs because they are not functional products, even at a minimal level. They are not *products* that are tested *in* the market; rather they are *prototypes* that are tested *with* the market. I call them mvps (minimum viable prototypes).

In Goodyear's eco-tire experiment, the prototype was a mock tire engraved with the "New Earth" logo, together with professional-looking marketing materials. In Pitney Bowes's small-scale metering machine experiment, the prototype was a web landing page with images showing the new device's capabilities.

In developing an MVP or an mvp, the prototype must be reduced to the minimal artifact necessary to conduct the experiment. The prototype itself does not need to meet any cost targets or requirements for performance or scalability or maintainability; it simply needs to support whatever experiment is being conducted.

## Pivot or Persist

After each experiment, the team must make a decision to pivot or persist (see Figure 2.3). To persist means to continue learning along the lines of the current plan; to pivot means to rethink a major element of the plan, such as the channel or an important aspect of the product. This discipline—to let data drive the pivot-or-persist decision—is at the heart of the Lean Startup method.

After the "New Earth" tire experiment, the team chose to pivot—in fact, to discontinue the initiative. In the case of Amita (the personal postage meter with custom images), the team used the experimental data to support a decision to persist—to proceed to product development.

There is no science to the pivot-or-persist decision; in the end, it is a judgment call, albeit one based on data. Some variant of the most recent

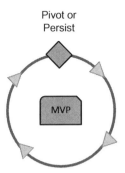

**FIGURE 2.3**
The pivot-or-persist decision

experiment that might overcome the negative results is always conceivable. The discipline of quick, well-considered experiments that yield objective data, however, generally leads to a consensus when the evidence is reviewed. That consensus may be a decision to stop an initiative, prompt the team to rethink several elements of the business model, or drive significant new investment to move the concept forward.

## THE INTEGRATIVE PRINCIPLE: INNOVATION ACCOUNTING

A Lean Startup team is focused on what needs to be true for a product to be successful in the market. Lean Learning Loops test the key assumptions about the business—one at a time. As the loops accumulate, however, the results of the business experiments must be tracked so that the team can hone its hypotheses and avoid repeating work. This tracking is what is meant by innovation accounting, and it is essential to progress. Innovation accounting provides a way of keeping track of progress when traditional measures like Stage-Gates or project milestones are not reliable indicators.

Innovation accounting may be carried out using a variety of tools. A Kanban board is a good way to track the status of the baseline assumptions (see Figure 2.4). Organizing the Kanban around the categories of Osterwalder's Business Model Canvas can be helpful, as well, to assure that you do not become too focused on one part of the business [Osterwalder and Pigneur, 2010] (see Figure 2.5). A portfolio view can help to track progress across initiatives. Whatever the structure, the tool must clearly

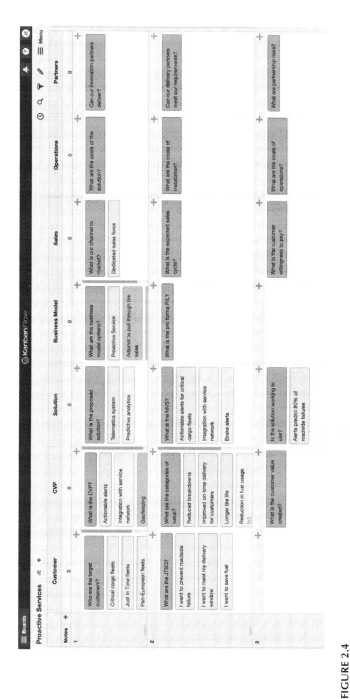

**FIGURE 2.4**

Tracking experiments with a Kanban board

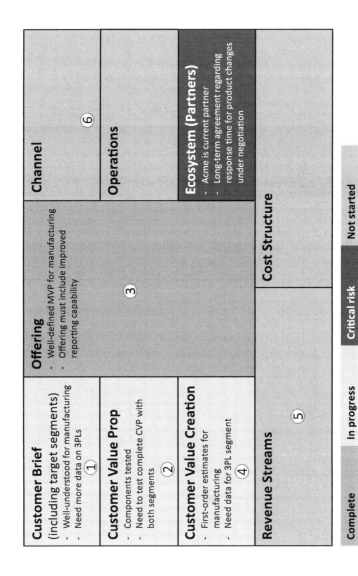

**FIGURE 2.5**
Status summary using a Business Model Canvas

associate the evidence gathered from an experiment with the hypothesis (or hypotheses) that it validates or invalidates. The team should meet regularly to review the status of the various experiments, make decisions to pivot or persist, and prioritize the next set of experiments.

Maintaining the discipline required for innovation accounting can be difficult. With so much going on, it can seem a distraction—and even a waste of time—to write everything down and to organize it in a Kanban or other tool. But innovation accounting is critical. If the practice is not followed, the team soon finds itself drifting into the urgencies of the day. The learning agenda is buried, and the team is no longer practicing Lean Startup.

## THE LAST THREE PRINCIPLES: WHAT TO LEARN

The last three principles deal with *what to learn*—the content of business building. These principles are represented as three key hypotheses: The Value Hypothesis, the Business Model Hypothesis, and the Growth Hypothesis.

### The Value Hypothesis

The Value Hypothesis captures the fit between the product or service concept and the market. The process of testing the Value Hypothesis goes by several names: Steve Blank calls the iterative process of creating the offering "customer development" [Blank, 2013], the Lean Product community talks about product-market fit [Olson, 2015], Eric Ries uses the term Value Hypothesis [Ries, 2011], in the design community, the term of art is "customer value proposition" [Lanning, 1998].

Whatever it is called, testing the Value Hypothesis (or crafting product-market fit) is very customer-intensive. It begins with a hypothesis about a customer need—what Clay [Christensen and Raynor, 2003] call a Job-to-be-Done (JTBD).

The validity of a JTBD is tested with a series of prototypes. The initial prototype is usually very simple—a storyboard, for example. Later versions may be more complex and complete, at least from the customer's perspective. A "Wizard of Oz" prototype, for example, appears to the user as a functioning product but is actually manipulated from behind the scenes. Ultimately, the test may require a prototype that the user can actually use—the MVP, as defined by Lean Startup.

Testing prototypes with customers and iteration over time assures that a customer need really exists and that the product concept could fulfill it—that is, that the product provides customer value. Geoffrey Moore provides a useful structure for defining the customer value proposition [Moore, 1991]:

- **For** <a customer segment>
- **Who** <experiences a specific problem (has a JTBD)>
- **We offer** <description of proposed solution>
- **Which delivers** <specific benefits>
- **Unlike competitive offers, our offer** <delivers important differentiators>.

This framing of the value proposition forces detailed consideration of all its key elements. Too often, a team can create a statement of the value proposition that may be very specific about the offering but is not as clear about the problem it solves or the benefits it delivers.

An example of a strong Value Hypothesis from the trucking industry, written in Moore's basic format, is:

> **For** *critical cargo fleets*
> **Who experience** *significant penalties from downtime due to roadside tire failure*
> **We offer** *intelligent monitoring of tires and predictive analytics*
> **Which deliver** *a reduction of over 80% in roadside failures due to poor tire maintenance*
> **Unlike competitive offers, our offer** (a) *provides actionable warnings and* (b) *is integrated with the service network.*

Note that this description is very specific with regard to the target customer, the issue to be resolved, and the way the customer's world will change as a result.

Another example, from the postal world:

> **For** *small businesses and individuals who currently use stamps*
> **Who seek to** *differentiate themselves in the eyes of their customers*
> **We offer** *a personal postage meter that can print custom stamp images*

**Which** *distinguishes the customer for branding or for special occasions*
**Unlike other offers, our offer** *lets you create your own, personalized stamp image.*

Again, the description is specific to each of the key elements. The specificity allows each of the elements to be tested before a major commitment is made to full development.

Any offering must create real customer value, tangible or intangible. It must be worth more to customers than it costs to produce and sell. If the equation doesn't balance properly, the product may be very desirable to customers but not economically feasible for the producer. Understanding the sources and magnitude of this value in very specific terms is part of developing the Value Hypothesis.

The Value Hypothesis is usually developed and tested using design methods. These methods are based on observational research (on-site insight), rapid prototyping of potential concepts, and iteration with potential users. Tom Kelley's books, *The Art of Innovation* and *The Ten Faces of Innovation*, provide a primer on design methods [Kelley, 2002, 2005].

## The Business Model Hypothesis

The Business Model Hypothesis is focused on how to capture value from a business concept. For a startup, creating a business model means starting from scratch, but for established companies, business model considerations can be more complex. In addition to being effective in the marketplace, the business model for the new concept must co-exist with the company's existing business model. Unfortunately, a truly new business idea will often not fit nicely into the existing model, and it cannot be shoehorned into it. Trying to force-fit a new concept into the dominant business model is a common recipe for failure—either failure to create a new business or failure to capture a fair share of the value created.

Getting the business model right is very important. Adrian Slywotzky notes that the difference in value capture for two firms meeting the same customer need but pursuing different business models can be as much as a factor of five [Slywotzky and Euchner, 2015]. I have found this to be true. One startup I worked with had a great offering but was selling it on a tiered subscription basis. When we did the math, we found that they were capturing only 3% of the value they created for their best customer. Refocusing the pricing around a gain-sharing model permitted a tripling in revenue.

Startups often use the Business Model Canvas to develop their business models [Osterwalder and Pigneur, 2010]. The canvas is useful in opening minds to new possibilities and for representing the elements of the business model. It gets good conversations going. But the Business Model Canvas cannot do several important things. First, because the elements are brainstormed independently, it does not assure the coherence of the business model—that is, it does not guarantee that the elements of the business model will synergistically support one another. Second, the canvas is not quantitative; the elements are there, but the canvas does not help to understand the viability or dynamics of the business model. Finally, competitors are off the canvas; as a result, the canvas does not deal with creating a competitive advantage, which is a key element of any business model.

The first business model that occurs to you—the obvious one—may very well not be the best one. Seeking alternatives and understanding the pros and cons of all the possibilities is important. I recommend that new ventures explore at least three alternative business models.

Business model archetypes are an excellent place to start. Entrepreneurs and researchers have identified several dozen archetypes, each of which assembles the elements in a coherent way and—if properly executed— creates economic leverage. In *The Art of Profitability*, Slywotzky explores the dynamics of 23 business model archetypes [Slywotzky, 2002]. Slywotzky has also written about *Profit Patterns* and *Value Migration* as industries move from one archetype to another. Oliver Gassmann and colleagues, in *The Business Model Navigator*, identified 54 quasi-archetypes [Gassmann et al., 2020]. Learning archetypal business models is extremely useful in selecting and adapting a model for your new venture.

As an example, Goodyear developed a technology that could use real-time data and predictive analytics to prevent over 80% of roadside failures due to tire maintenance issues in truck fleets (see above). In creating the Business Model Hypothesis for the project, the team looked at three alternatives. One business model bundled the service with tire sales and generated profit via pull-through of a product; another model sold the component parts of the system to fleets so that they could implement the system themselves; a third charged for the service on a subscription model and provided the service for both Goodyear and competitor tires.

We analyzed the risks of each model and ultimately chose the third, which represented a marked departure from the product-centric business model of the core business. This model required a different approach to selling, a different revenue model, and different metrics than the company was accustomed to. Pull-through of tires was a consequence but not the driver. When we analyzed the economics and the risks, it was the only model that we believed would be sustainable. This model has enabled the business to grow and has been adapted to markets throughout the world.

## The Growth Hypothesis

The Growth Hypothesis is a theory for how the business will scale. In startups, scale often happens organically: As sales increase, the startup reconfigures itself to manage them and seeks investment to accelerate growth. This often requires a significant infusion of cash to properly fund the elements of the business necessary for growth. Investments in the sales force, in infrastructure, in operations personnel, and in technology are often required. Moving too slowly or investing too little may mean that the venture misses its window of opportunity.

In established corporations, the Growth Hypothesis is often developed and validated in a distinct step: *Incubation.* Incubation has the advantage of testing the whole business proposition at a small scale and low risk. It validates first and foremost that customers will buy the offering at a price sufficient to sustain the business and, therefore, that the business can be made profitable.

Once profitability has been demonstrated, many options are available for achieving scale. In a large company, the options include investment for organic growth, reorganization of parts of the existing business to serve as a basis for the new venture, and acquisition—or a combination of all of these. The business-building strategy is, in essence, the validated Growth Hypothesis (see Figure 2.6).

For example, a company that had developed a new document management system for hospitals considered three options to drive growth. The first two envisioned building the business organically but with different levels of investment. In the first, a plan was developed to maximize value, which included substantial investment. In the second, the team sought to minimize cash-flow requirements and to grow incrementally. The third option was to build the business by acquiring another business with complementary capabilities. The acquired business would provide access to a customer base and a means of making the acquired business more profitable. The innovation team developed full financial projections for each option, as well as an analysis of the risks of each. These projections provided the basis for the scale decision.

The assumptions inherent in a Growth Hypothesis need to be tested with customers, just as the elements of the business model are tested. In the end, however, the decision about growth is constrained by two things: The economic dynamics of the business and the leadership team's risk profile. Many internal ventures succeed or fail based on the willingness of executives to invest sufficiently in growth.

The Lean Startup is a system. Each of the elements is attractive as a stand-alone practice, but the value for new business innovation comes from adopting Lean Startup in its entirety. Developing MVPs without systematically testing them through Lean Learning Loops misses critical customer feedback. Developing radically new value propositions and then forcing them through an existing business model can make a viable business fail. Doing the work without a learning-based management system devolves into assessment by more traditional metrics and can lead to shortsighted decisions. Although the Lean Startup tools are each useful in thinking about innovation, it is the integration of them that leads to success.

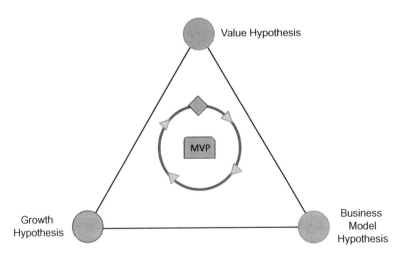

**FIGURE 2.6**
The key hypotheses

# 3

## *What's Different in Large Organizations: Why Lean Startup Is Not Enough*

Steve Blank, one of the founders of the Lean Startup movement, said that his first big Aha! was the realization that startups are not just smaller versions of large companies [Blank and Euchner, 2018]. For years, he had watched entrepreneurs and venture capitalists try to manage startups using the tools that are common in successful established enterprises— the business plan, stage-and-gate product development practices, and evaluation through the P&L statement. Blank and his collaborators realized these tools were not appropriate for the context that startups operate in. This is because they do not accommodate the conditions of extreme uncertainty that characterize the world that startups operate in—uncertainty about customers' emerging needs, uncertainty about the market, uncertainty about technology, and uncertainty about costs. The Lean Startup methodology was designed to deal with these uncertainties by creating a learning organization that can deal with extreme uncertainty productively and systematically.

Lean Startup is appealing to large companies engaging in new business innovation for precisely the same reasons. But just as a startup is not a smaller version of a large company, an internal venture in a large company is not just a startup that happens to be hosted in an established enterprise. The corporate environment makes all the difference—both positive and negative. The differences—which are significant—can be managed, and even leveraged to support success. But making Lean Startup work in corporate settings requires conscious management of the differences.

DOI: 10.4324/9780429433887-3

---

## YES ... AND

Ironically, the methods of Lean Startup can often trigger antibodies in a company, so that the corporate body rejects the new organism. In fact, each of the elements of the Lean Startup creates its own reaction. These antibodies all are rooted in real threats to the core business, and as with the human body, each of the antibody reactions acts in some way to protect the host organism. At the same time, each of the antibody reactions is to some extent irrational, based more on fear than on reason. If the risks are properly managed, however, the fears can be overcome and Lean Startup can be successful in the corporate context.

There are seven key differences that drive this resistance, the first six of which are associated with Lean Startup practices. The seventh addresses the difference in the investment context for a corporate executive vs. a venture capitalist investing in a startup. These differences must be managed for the Lean Startup method to succeed in corporate settings. The Lean Startup practices, the risks that they pose, and the fears that they induce are captured in Table 3.1.

To manage these risks (and fears), internal ventures must implement practices to address them. Each of the seven risks is discussed at a high level below. Successful practices for managing them are explored in the following chapters.

### 1. The Need to Contain the Chaos

The Lean Startup methodology is somewhat chaotic. It works, when it works well, because the chaos is managed through a learning agenda. Over the course of a weekly sprint, many things can change: The feature set of a Minimum Viable Product (MVP), the target customer, the channel to market, or the revenue model, for example. In the context of a typical business process, these rapid, interrelated changes look like they are unmanaged. Even with frequent reviews and good documentation of the decisions made as a result, the iterative nature of Lean Startup and the many small, targeted efforts can look undirected, and even random. Progress emerges from this chaos, but it is not always obvious to those outside the process.

**TABLE 3.1**

The Risks of Lean Startup in Existing Organizations

| Lean Startup | Legitimate Concern | Fear |
|---|---|---|
| Iterate using **Lean Learning Loops: Pivot or Persist** | An unmanaged process | Chaos |
| Develop an **MVP** to get market feedback quickly | Distraction of the functions that make the core efficient | Loss of control |
| Develop the **Value Hypothesis** | Pursuing opportunities that the company cannot exploit (orphans) | Loss of identity |
| Develop the **Business Model Hypothesis** | Cannibalization of the core | Undermining the business |
| Create a **Growth Hypothesis** and build an organization that can scale | Misallocation of resources | Draining of needed resources from the core |
| **Innovation Accounting** based on a learning agenda | Failure to assess new ventures rigorously | Making a blunder |
| **Bet to win** | Failure to manage the expectations of Wall Street | Getting fired |

Product innovation in large organizations is typically more linear and is managed through a defined, staged process. As a result, executive leadership teams are conditioned to expect a more predictable process, and they often struggle to discern the progress in Lean Startup's messy iterations. They want a more linear indicator of progress.

An Innovation Stage-Gate can provide the needed bridge. The stages provide reasonable estimates of the timeframes for achieving key milestones, and each stage culminates in a defined set of intermediate deliverables. At the level of a gate deliverable, the process looks defined and (somewhat) predictable, in a way analogous to the traditional stage-and-gate product development processes that many organizations use. *Within* each of the stages, however, Lean Startup methods reign; the process is agile, dynamic, and a bit chaotic.

The Lean Startup approach does not fit seamlessly into such a model. An Innovation Stage-Gate by its nature separates in time some of the activities that might be undertaken simultaneously in the Lean Startup approach. As an example, customer insight and the development of the customer value proposition (CVP) can be usefully separated from creation of the business model—and in the context of corporate innovation, it is often helpful to do so. Similarly, development of the business model can be separated from in-market incubation of the concept, reducing the risks of entering the market with an untested offering. Finally, the decision to scale the venture can be separated from the decision to incubate it. This separation makes sense because, at least inside a corporation, the decision to scale is a distinct, purposeful act, not an opportunistic evolution.

A stage-and-gate process like this may strike some as antithetical to the Lean Startup approach, and even to innovation itself. It is, however, a critical element of making the match between Lean Startup and corporate culture. It provides the clear sense of progress that corporate leaders want, introduces major gates at which investment decisions can be made, and creates a space where executives can learn, over time, about a new market, its risks, and its promise.

Startups need only be concerned with creating a fit with the market. An internal venture, on the other hand, needs to worry, as well, about managing the expectations of internal stakeholders. Chapter 4 discusses Innovation Stage-Gates and how they work.

## 2. The Need to Manage Disruptions to Operations

Every company has what Vijay Govindarajan and Chris Trimble call a "performance engine"—the collection of functions, processes, and resources that have been optimized over time to maximize the success and profitability of the core business [Govindarajan and Euchner, 2010]. The key functions include sales, marketing, intellectual property law, procurement, IT, and liability. The people who work in these functions have defined objectives and internal client expectations; they also have skills, capabilities, and methods of operating that have been honed to meet the needs of the current business. An innovation team—especially one focused on breakthrough innovation—can disrupt this finely tuned machine. How does one deal with this dilemma?

Some innovation experts recommend creating an entirely independent entity, with its own HR, IT, procurement, legal, and engineering functions, to maintain a buffer between the new venture and the performance engine. This approach is expensive, however, and in many cases impractical. Other organizations require the venture to use the corporation's existing functions and attempt to use pressure from the top to get things done. When the performance engine cannot or will not provide what the venture needs, the venture team goes to its corporate sponsors to force the issue. This approach works well until the escalation practice wears thin; then it tends to collapse, often with long-term consequences for the innovation function.

There is a third way, one that engages the corporation's functions in a transparent but graduated way. This allows the venture to benefit from corporate resources without creating unnecessary disruption for the performance engine. Purposively engaging the organization and seeking partnership takes time; it requires planning, open communication, and real compromise on important issues. But it can enable an internal venture to work constructively with functions and to leverage their rich knowledge and resources.

A startup—even one fortunate enough to be part of an accelerator—does not have such resources available to it, but neither does it have the challenge of coordinating with a resistant core business. Chapter 5 discusses the frictions and corporate games that surround working with the performance engine. It introduces "Graduated Engagement," a practical tool for productive co-existence.

## 3. The Need for Strategic Alignment

Corporations have defined strategies, whether they are explicitly stated or implicitly enacted. Any new venture must align with these strategies or with an explicitly espoused growth strategy. This is true even if the CEO says there are no bounds on the innovation team and that he or she will invest in any truly good new venture. For a variety of reasons, this promise is almost never true. If executives cannot see the connection to a larger objective – if the focus area of the innovation is not relevant to a larger goal – it is unlikely that key decision-makers will take the time to understand the new domain in sufficient depth to make decisions with confidence. Said another way, if the new venture is perceived as diverting resources from the existing corporate strategy rather than moving it forward, then investment will not flow. For this reason, internal ventures must find ways to align themselves with the broader corporate strategy. The innovation platform must make sense not only in the competitive world; it must make sense for the company.

This alignment can be difficult to achieve for a variety of reasons. The most common reason is that the growth strategy beyond the core is so rarely articulated. As a result, any connection to the core business can be lost. Vijay Govindarajan estimates that, for an internal venture to succeed, 40% of its critical assets must build on the assets of the core business [Govindarajan and Euchner, 2010]. If the new venture does not leverage the core assets of the corporation, then the disadvantages of being part of a corporation will outweigh its advantages, and the venture will fail.

Asset-based opportunity spaces are a means for creating alignment. An asset-based opportunity space is defined by the intersection of market opportunity and some set of corporate assets. Such intersections provide a fertile hunting ground for growth. Trends in technology, demographics, and consumer expectations create areas of opportunity; leveraging existing assets in new ways creates the right to win. Success requires both flexibility of thought about the value of existing assets and an unusual capacity for sharing them.

The process of identifying asset-based opportunity spaces is idiosyncratic. In some instances, it starts by considering an asset in a new light and asking how it might be repurposed. Williams Pipeline's re-envisioning of its unused natural gas pipelines as conduit for a telecommunications network is a great example. At other times, it can start with a clear market opportunity, which is looked at through the lens of corporate assets. In this instance, the assets provide a basis for competitive advantage. In other instances, there will be signals from the market that suggest a new use of an asset. Potential customers may be asking for an offering that you have not yet considered but that leverages your capabilities.

Chapter 6 discusses how to think about assets and opportunities. It includes an interview with John Rossman, formerly of Amazon, which is a master at asset-based innovation [Rossman and Euchner, 2018].

Startups do not have to align with any external strategy, nor do they benefit from the use of existing assets.

## 4. The Need to Introduce a New Business Model

A business model is a configuration of resources, assets, and processes designed to profitably deliver a customer value proposition. A good business model creates differentiation in the marketplace and has economic leverage—it gets better with scale.

Over time, a company's dominant business model, like its performance engine, is optimized. When a company reaches this stage, it has internalized a core set of assumptions that drive important decisions, especially those about resource allocation. As a result, the dominant business model in any corporation always looms large. It is easy to work in alignment with it but very difficult to challenge its assumptions.

Introducing a new business model is both costly and risky. It means going back to square one and learning anew how to drive profitability. At the same time, a new business model threatens the existing business model. A major concern is whether the new business will cannibalize the old, resulting in a net loss for the corporation. Another is that it will disrupt relationships with partners that make the core business successful. A third is that it will distract attention from the core business and sap resources from it.

Because the dominant business model is so difficult to challenge, corporations often attempt to force radical new value propositions to market through their existing business model (or a slight variant of it). This impulse can lead to two types of problems. First, the venture may simply fail: Delivering the value proposition effectively through the dominant model may simply not be economically possible. Alternately, the old business model may appear to work, but it may be unable to capture sufficient value for the benefits it delivers; the business may succeed but leave much of the value created on the table.

To be successful, any new venture needs to consider a range of business model alternatives and to force itself to think outside the box. Business model archetypes are an effective starting place. Chapter 7 discusses the Business Model Pyramid and a step-by-step approach for introducing a new business model to an existing corporation. It includes an interview with Adrian Slywotzky, whose concept of the business model archetype is at the center of the method [Slywotzky and Euchner, 2015].

Startups do not face the dilemma of co-existing with a dominant business model. They do not have anything in place either to constrain or support them.

## 5. The Need to Protect the NewCo

Organizational issues do not loom large when an internal venture is small. Everyone involved does whatever is necessary for success. Resources are begged, borrowed, stolen, and cajoled into being. This is true for startups as well, although the sources of resources are different.

As the venture matures, however, both startups and internal ventures need to manage a new set of challenges. In both cases, for example, the leadership may need to change as the venture enters its growth stage. The team itself must often be reshaped as well in order to take full advantage of the opportunity that has been created.

An internal venture must address an additional set of issues. When it was small, it could fly under the radar. As long as it was able to muster the resources it needed, it could operate and learn. But growth changes things. It makes the challenges the venture creates for the *status quo* visible. The core often fights back (especially if it feels it has the political permission to do so).

Moving the venture from incubation to scale must be done carefully, especially if the new business intends to leverage the assets of the core business. Internal ventures often fail because the balance is poorly made: The integration is too tight to accommodate the differences in business models or too loose to enable leveraging of corporate assets. The Separate-but-Connected Model developed by Govindarajan and Trimble is a useful construct [Govindarajan and Trimble, 2010]. It provides for an independent new venture but with clearly negotiated interfaces with the core business. Organizing for Growth is discussed in Chapter 8, which includes an interview with Vijay Govindarajan [Govindarajan and Euchner, 2010].

Startups do not need to manage the risks of the host corporation's response to a venture's growth; internal ventures do.

## 6. The Need to Bet to Win

Once a startup has been brought to the point where it has been proven to be attractive to customers, profitable, and scalable, a venture capitalist will go all-in to win in the marketplace. But the corporate investor, confronted with alternate investment paths, will often choose the one that minimizes the downside risk rather than the one that maximizes the venture's potential. This is understandable. It can be hard for a public company to explain to Wall Street that a dip in earnings is due to significant investment in a new and very different business.

Making these bets requires a different kind of leader—one that Michael Tushman refers to as an "ambidextrous leader" [O'Reilly and Tushman, 2004]. An ambidextrous leader is able to both operate an ongoing business successfully (*exploit* an existing business) and create new avenues for growth (*explore* new businesses). Learning to be ambidextrous is difficult because the attributes of the two leadership styles are very different—and often conflict with one another. It is important for leaders to learn how to shift their mindsets as the circumstances require. Chapter 9 discusses ambidextrous leadership and some tools that can help to encourage it. It includes excerpts of an interview with Michael Tushman [Tushman and Euchner, 2015].

Startups are in the business of exploration and growth; they do not have to worry about optimizing operations (at least not yet).

## SUMMARY

Lean Startup is an effective set of practices for creating new businesses. It provides a set of seven principles that, taken together, manage the conditions of extreme uncertainty under which a startup must operate. The principles are not enough for new ventures that are housed inside an existing corporation, however. Succeeding in a corporate context requires a complementary set of practices for managing the relationship between the core business and the new venture.

The balance of this book is devoted to a set of practices that have been successful in making Lean Startup work in corporate contexts. Each chapter discusses a Lean Startup principle, the issues that it raises inside the corporate context, and specific tools for managing them.

The issues considered in this book are not new. In many cases, they have been studied in isolation by academicians and other thought leaders who have studied corporate innovation. What is new is their integration with Lean Startup principles in order to create a holistic system for corporate innovation.

These are "Yes … And" practices. To succeed, internal ventures must pursue Lean Startup practices *and* complement them with practices to address the particular risks and challenges of the corporate context. Table 3.2 outlines the complementary practices and serves as an outline for the rest of the book.

**TABLE 3.2**

Yes … And: Complementary Practices to Make Lean Startup Work in a Large Organization

| Lean Startup | And | Lean Startup in Large Organizations |
|---|---|---|
| Iterate using **Lean Learning Loops** | … | Contain the chaos with an **Innovation Stage-Gate** |
| Develop a **Minimum Viable Product** to get market feedback quickly | … | Use **Graduated Engagement** to minimize resistance from the performance engine |
| Develop the **Value Hypothesis** | … | Focus on **Asset-Based Opportunity Spaces** in order to achieve strategic alignment |
| Develop the **Business Model Hypothesis** | … | Consider alternative business models using the **Business Model Pyramid**; seek a model that provides both market fit and corporate fit |
| Create the **Growth Hypothesis** and build an organization that can scale | … | Organize to protect the venture from internal political pressures using the **Separate-but-Connected Model** |
| Use **Innovation Accounting** to measure learning to reduce market uncertainty and risk | … | Develop **Ambidextrous Leaders** who can manage both the exploitation of the core business and exploration of new businesses |

# 4

## Containing the Chaos: An Innovation Stage-Gate

### LEAN LEARNING LOOPS AND A PERCEPTION OF CHAOS

Lean Learning Loops are at the very heart of the Lean Startup method. In the Lean Startup, in fact, the process of innovation is nothing more than a sequence of Lean Learning Loops: Stating a hypothesis, designing an experiment to test it, running the experiment, and reviewing the results to decide whether to pivot or persist.

The Lean Startup's combination of experimental approaches, successive prototypes, and feedback-driven pivots can seem like chaos inside a company—and antithetical to the disciplined, time-tested processes most companies use to drive new product development.

Although many executives will acknowledge that new business innovation is inherently different from the development of next-generation products, the Lean Startup practices can seem like a bridge too far. Where are the checkpoints? How do we ensure that we get input from all the relevant stakeholders? How do we know that what we are investing in will work? Why would we want to institutionalize rework?

Faced with the challenge of new venture innovation, executives can feel caught in a dilemma: Whether to manage innovation through an inappropriate but manageable process or cede control to what looks like unmanaged—and maybe unmanageable—chaos.

An Innovation Stage-Gate offers one resolution to this dilemma. By containing the Lean Startup learning cycles within defined stages and by establishing gates with intermediate deliverables, an Innovation Stage-Gate can capture the best of both worlds: It can permit exploration

DOI: 10.4324/9780429433887-4

and iterative learning to co-exist with the defined process that most corporations demand.

---

## THE INNOVATION STAGE-GATE

The Innovation Stage-Gate is an adaptation of the standard Stage-Gate product development process, originally developed by Bob Cooper and colleagues [Cooper, et al., 2002a, 2002b]. The use of the Stage-Gate has become the gold standard in corporate product development processes, where it is used to manage alignment, budgets, schedules, and stakeholder input for new product development. When Stage-Gate™ systems are implemented well, they are cross-functional, incorporating representation and input throughout the product development process from all key functions: Engineering, Marketing, Sales, Service, R&D, Finance, and IT.

In a Stage-Gate™ system, new product development moves through a serial process: Beginning with requirements and moving from high-level design to detailed design, implementation, testing, launch, and finally post-launch assessment. Review occurs at the gates that mark the end of each phase. The review process provides opportunities for each function to raise concerns as the project develops, and it assures that resources are appropriately allocated across functions to support agreed-upon objectives. A key benefit of the Stage-Gate™ approach is the alignment of objectives, resources, and timing across the company. Periodic, defined review points provide assurance to all that the larger investments required in the later, more expensive phases of the project will only be made if key risks are addressed in the earlier stages.

Implementing such a process—and maintaining its discipline—is usually organizationally difficult. A Stage-Gate™ requires people to defend their decisions to a larger audience, to make public commitments, and to take on work to prepare for meetings, all of which people naturally resist. If exceptions are permitted, they become the rule, so managers of Stage-Gate™ often brook no exceptions. The Stage-Gate™ approach has a history of working well for new product development within existing businesses; it is, in fact, the core innovation practice in most industrial corporations.

The traditional Stage-Gate™ does not work well for startups, however. This is because it assumes clarity at the start—clarity about customers and their needs, about timelines, about business models, and about budgets. This clarity just doesn't exist for a startup. The baseline questions of what will be built, for whom, and (at least roughly) with what resources simply cannot be answered for new ventures, which operate under conditions of much greater uncertainty than is present in traditional product development. For the startup, everything is unknown. Lean Startup is designed to accommodate that uncertainty through an iterative learning approach.

At first glance, Lean Startup and Stage-Gate™ can seem antithetical. Lean Startup is focused on the rapid iteration of a new business concept to find a fit with the market, a process that might be termed *successive elaboration* (aspects of all the stages happen simultaneously). This is in contrast to a traditional Stage-Gate™, which generally follows a process of *successive refinement* (the target concept becomes more fully developed at each stage). The Innovation Stage-Gate seeks to bridge the two and to address the concerns that naturally arise with Lean Startup.

Conflicts may arise from several sources. There may be basic business concerns (for instance, whether ventures of this sort are a good use of the company's resources) or organizational issues (uncertainty about who in the organization should be accountable for the venture and its innovations). There may be strategic concerns (whether the team is working in the most appropriate opportunity spaces) or methodological concerns (whether the venture's approach to innovation even makes sense). The Innovation Stage-Gate seeks to resolve these issues by containing the chaos inside well-defined stages.

In many ways, the Innovation Stage-Gate™ is simply an unraveling of the key areas of focus in the Lean Startup triangle. The Value Hypothesis, the Business Model Hypothesis, and the Growth Hypothesis become gates, worked on sequentially rather than all at once. Lean Learning Loops happen within all of the stages, with different sets of assumptions and different types of MVPs. As with traditional Stage-Gate™, the gates provide opportunities for managerial oversight, staged release of funds, and cross-organizational input.

Figure 4.1 provides an example of such a process, one that has been successfully implemented at Goodyear Tire & Rubber Company [Ganguly and Euchner, 2018]. This version of an Innovation Stage-Gate™ system starts with defining clear opportunity spaces (Phase I); uses design methods to discover new ways of creating customer value (Phase II); considers different

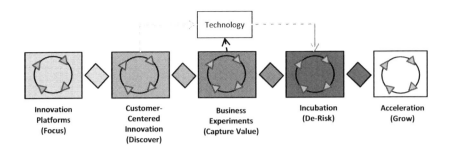

**FIGURE 4.1**
An Innovation Stage-Gate

business models for capturing value (Phase III); and incubates the business at a small scale (Phase IV), before fully launching the business (Phase V). Each of these phases brings distinct challenges for internal ventures and for the corporations that host them.

The first two phases develop the venture's Value Hypothesis. In Phase I, the venture team focuses on identifying appropriate innovation platforms. This phase addresses the need for strategic alignment; it assures that the innovation team is fishing in waters that matter for the company as a whole. The work in this phase produces a clear statement of domains within which the company would like to innovate, and why.

Phase II focuses on developing the customer value proposition (CVP). The work in this phase anchors the venture in a deep understanding of customer needs. The focus on the customer prevents distractions; it keeps the team from wandering around the wilderness. Customer focus also helps established companies to unlock from things that they think that they know (which just don't happen to be true) and to explore opportunities with new eyes. The deliverables for this phase are a customer brief, a value proposition that responds to targeted needs in that brief, and an estimate of the customer value that will be created with the value proposition.

In Phase III, the focus shifts to the Business Model Hypothesis. The main challenge to a new venture within an established business is the company's tendency to default to its core business model—and to actively resist new business models. The goal of work in this phase is to explore the range of alternatives, test business models appropriate to the CVP, and select the one that delivers the most value. This work includes experiments that are conducted "with-market" (before the business is incubated), not "in-market." With-market experiments are conducted out in the real world, with real people and in real contexts. They are usually focused on specific issues necessary for success, not on the overall viability of the business. Business experiments accelerate learning at low risk. The deliverables for the business model phase are the identification of a few alternative business models, a risk analysis for each model, and a profit and loss statement for a single customer that demonstrates the viability of the business.

Once the CVP and business model are identified, the venture begins developing its Growth Hypothesis. In Phase IV, the Incubation phase, the business is tested in-market, on a small scale. The purposes of incubation are to validate the business model in the real world and to develop alternative Growth Hypotheses. Critically, the learning that happens in incubation also helps to clarify any risks to the core business. For incubation to be effective, it must be managed with governance mechanisms that keep the focus on learning. The key deliverables are the demonstration of profitability in practice and the development of alternative growth plans to build the business.

Finally, in Phase V, the venture turns its attention to scale. This is the point at which many internal ventures fail. Executing a growth plan often requires, in addition to capital, the ability to leverage key assets of the parent corporation. This need creates the potential for significant conflict and political threats to the new venture. Unfortunately, many ventures are smothered by the core business or starved of resources because insufficient planning is devoted to organizing for scale. The deliverable for this stage is a specific plan for scale, including a clear negotiation of the roles and rights of the new venture in relation to the core.

Each stage of an Innovation Stage-Gate is characterized by iteration. At each step, many hypotheses, of different types, are posited and proven or disproven. The process relies on Lean Learning Loops using prototypes (though not necessarily MVPs) to test clearly stated hypotheses. It can feel chaotic and hard to track. The results at one stage may require cycling back to earlier phases (although this is less common if the earlier stages have been thoroughly developed and tested). Pivots are still relevant, but they take place within a phase.

The entire focus of an Innovation Stage-Gate is learning: Learning about customer needs and new ways of meeting them; learning about business risks and how to allay them; and learning about the business in the market before moving to scale. Many ideas fall by the wayside during the process, as assumptions about the world and about the business are disconfirmed. But if an innovation team is deliberate and honest with itself, real opportunities emerge. An Innovation Stage-Gate provides the framework for this learning, one that lets it happen within a traditional corporate structure.

## INNOVATION STAGE-GATE DELIVERABLES

Like a traditional Stage-Gate, the gates of the Innovation Stage-Gate are associated with specific deliverables that are reviewed before the project moves to the next phase. An Innovation Stage-Gate developed at Goodyear demonstrates what kinds of deliverables are useful.

### FOCUS

The first phase of the Innovation Stage-Gate is Focus. At this stage, the innovation team is concerned with defining an opportunity space that makes sense for the company. The opportunity space depends on the target industry, on general trends affecting that industry, and on the potential of emerging technologies to disrupt current ways of serving customers. A corporation is likely to be more successful—and has more of a right to win—if it considers the opportunity space in terms of the assets it brings to the table, as well. Those assets may include brand, existing distribution capabilities, technical know-how, an established customer base, or an infrastructure that can be used for new ventures. A good innovation practice considers the potential to repurpose assets to create a competitive advantage.

Within any opportunity space is a large set of potential *strategic questions*. A strategic question defines the particular corner of the opportunity space that the innovation team will explore during a given engagement. It needs to include enough definition to define the perceived problem; clarity about who, in particular, experiences that problem; and why it might be a good time to reexamine current ways of doing things. A good strategic question is focused but provisional. As the team learns, the question may be refined. It is, however, an essential starting point.

One example of a strategic question is, "How can our company use digital tools to improve document management practices in community hospitals?" Another might be, "How can we use digital technology to help commercial trucking fleets improve uptime?" Each of these strategic questions defines (in a very broad sense) the specific customer (community hospitals, commercial trucking fleets); what is new (digital technology); and the problem space that needs to be addressed (document management, uptime).

The deliverables at this phase of development are (1) a clear *Point of View* about the future and (2) a set of well-developed *strategic questions* based on the Point of View.

## VALUE CREATION

The second phase in the Innovation Stage-Gate, Discovery, is focused on the creation of new customer value. During this phase, the team seeks to identify and validate important unmet customer needs, especially those that might be met in new ways with the emergence of new capabilities.

The focus during this phase is entirely on creating customer value (not on capturing value for the company). Customer insight works best when it follows the practices of design [see Kelley, 2002, 2005]. Design starts with careful observation of customers in their natural habitat, often using the tools of ethnography to uncover important unmet customer needs.

Once the team has a good idea about who its customers are and what they need, it moves on to developing a Customer Value Proposition (CVP). The CVP is developed by looking creatively across the set of validated customer needs and focusing on the most important of them. The goal of a CVP is to solve a problem for a specific customer set that matters. A good CVP has the form:

- For <a customer segment>,
- Who <is experiencing a specific problem>,
- We offer <description of proposed solution>,
- Which delivers <specific benefits>,
- Unlike competitive offers, our offer <cite important differentiators>.

The CVP should be tested with the targeted customer set using some form of prototype before proceeding to later stages.

A CVP may appear to be perfect for the market, and it may have gotten great feedback. But before proceeding to develop a business model, the team should estimate the *customer value* that the CVP actually creates. Without this knowledge, it will not be clear which business models are viable and which of them are capable of capturing fair value for the company. Customer value creation can be estimated in three steps:

(a) Identify categories of value creation, such as lower costs, faster cycle time, improved quality, reduced inventory, increased customer satisfaction, or others.

(b) Estimate the range of value created in each category. These numbers will, by necessity, be a bit rough, but they set the bounds of potential value created.

(c) Develop the value equation (which aggregates the value in quantitative terms). Once the value equation is written, it can be instantiated with data on the current state and with estimates of the potential value creation in dollar terms.

The deliverables at the Value Creation phase include (1) a *Customer Brief* that describes in some detail the customers, their personas, and their most compelling needs, (2) the *Customer Value Proposition*, and (3) an estimate of *Customer Value Creation*.

## VALUE CAPTURE

The amount of value captured for a given value proposition will depend heavily on the business model adopted. The difference in value capture can be as much as a factor of five for different business models used to address the same customer problem. It is valuable to consider multiple business model alternatives in some depth prior to settling on the one to implement.

The first deliverable in this phase therefore is the identification of at least three *alternative business models*, together with the pros and cons of each. Rough financial models can illuminate which model might have the most financial leverage. Once the alternative models have all been studied, the team selects one for detailed risk analysis and modeling.

The second deliverable in this phase is a business case but not a traditional business case. It is useful at this stage to develop a *Single Customer P&L*. The Single Customer P&L is focused on understanding what it will take to make the business profitable. It is concrete, in that it focuses on a single customer or type of customer, and it provides a base from which the business's potential can be extrapolated. This intermediate business case can require a lot of experimentation, but the insight it yields is well worth the time.

The *Case for Incubation* builds on the Single Customer P&L to show the potential of the business for the company. It summarizes the business proposition, the business model that will be pursued, what has been learned to reduce the risk of that business model, and what is still to be learned. The incubation case is what launches the business into the market on a small scale.

The deliverables at the Value Capture phase include (1) *three alternative business models*, (2) the *Single Customer P&L*, and (3) the *Case for Incubation*.

## INCUBATION

Incubation is entering the market at a manageable scale. It answers two questions: (1) Is the business profitable in practice? and (2) is there a viable plan for bringing the business to scale? The data on sales, profits, and lessons learned in the test market answer the first question. The answer to the second question depends on decisions about how to build the business. Alternative scenarios can help illuminate the best path. For instance, the team may wish to include in the analysis a scenario that minimizes losses as the business grows, a scenario that maximizes market potential, and a scenario that builds the business through acquisition or partnerships.

Incubation is often the longest phase, as the team works to acquire customers and develop the operations necessary for long-term success. The deliverables of the Incubation phase are: (1) *a P&L demonstrating that the business will be profitable*, once it is brought to scale, and (2) *alternative business-building strategies*.

## STAFFING THE INNOVATION STAGE-GATE

Making an Innovation Stage-Gate work in practice takes people with the skills and resources to succeed. Gina O'Connor, who focuses on *"The People Side of Breakthrough Innovation,"* has mapped out the skills innovators must have in two dimensions. The first dimension of her matrix deals with the organization. It includes the working level, the platform (opportunity space) level, and the portfolio (executive) level. The second dimension deals with the innovation process, which she divides into three stages: Discovery, Incubation, and Acceleration. Discovery includes the Focus and Value Creation phases above; Incubation includes both the Value Capture and Incubation phases; and Acceleration is focused on bringing the venture to scale (see Figure 4.2).

O'Connor has observed that notably different skills are required in each of the phases of innovation, which is why she has structured the process as she has. The skills of Discovery are primarily drawn from the disciplines of foresight and design. The skills for Incubation are drawn from the disciplines of business and entrepreneurship and include the practices of Lean Startup. The skills for Acceleration are those required for sales and operations.

O'Connor's main point is very clear: Inside large companies, you need to establish and staff an innovation management system based on an Innovation Stage-Gate. Without such a system, you may occasionally succeed, by dint of the will of a few extraordinary people and a bit of luck. But with a well-staffed and managed innovation function, you create the potential for sustained and repeatable success. An excerpt of my interview with Gina O'Connor is included in this chapter [O'Connor and Euchner, 2017].

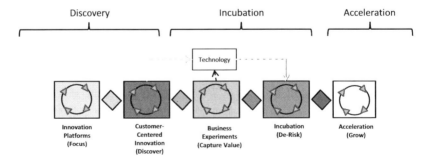

**FIGURE 4.2**
O'Connor's innovation stages

## KEY INSIGHTS

- Lean Startup practices can collide with some of the norms of large enterprises
- An Innovation Stage-Gate can contain the chaos and provide the benefits of both worlds
- Success requires staffing the innovation function with people who have different skills for the different phases of the Stage-Gate
- A management system based on an Innovation Stage-Gate and staffed appropriately enables repeatable success.

### THE PEOPLE SIDE OF BREAKTHROUGH INNOVATION

### AN INTERVIEW WITH GINA O'CONNOR

[We] know from the entrepreneurship literature and the behavior of the venture capital world that people who are really good at starting things often aren't good at running high-growth businesses and certainly are not good at maintaining mature businesses. There are different skills required at different stages of an innovation ...

The most important thing [for a company] is to define the roles that are required for innovation and the skills those roles require. Lack of role clarity, or role ambiguity, is a huge topic of research in the academic literature. It is critically important to employee satisfaction, morale, and performance. Role ambiguity is a huge problem in the innovation space ...

If you want to build a sustainable capability, we have found that there are nine more or less distinct roles that need to be filled. We represent them as a matrix. There are two dimensions of this matrix. The first [dimension of the matrix covers] the three innovation capabilities that we identified in our earlier research and described in *Grabbing Lightning*: discovery, incubation, and acceleration. The second [dimension] relates to hierarchy or scope: innovation is managed at the project level, the platform level, and the portfolio level. The cells define nine roles ...

Once the roles are clear, we can talk about how an organization can manage to fill them even with fewer resources. We're not trying to fill positions here but clarify the roles. This level of specificity is really helpful even if a given organization may have one person ful-filling multiple roles ...

[There are two leadership roles that span across the matrix]. One is what we call the Orchestrator; that's like the COO of the innovation function. The other is the Chief Innovation Officer. The Orchestrator manages the portfolio. He is focused within the innovation func-tion, making sure that project teams are staffed correctly and that the portfolio is balanced across discovery, incubation, and accelera-tion. He assures that the processes that we're using are working well and is helping to create a network with middle management in the business units as projects need them ...

[The Chief Innovation Officer is] managing the linkage at the senior level. He's a member of the C-suite, the executive team. He's managing the connection to the growth strategy: if you don't have a clear sense of strategic intent for the future, you won't be very suc-cessful at breakthrough innovation ...

There is a pipeline of initiatives to support the strategic platforms you have chosen. Companies that are successful with this have a head of the Discovery portfolio, a head of the Incubation portfolio, and leadership of the businesses in Acceleration ...

[The people in these roles are different types. The Discovery peo-ple] ... like the big picture: everything is open and everything's con-nected and it's cool. The guys in Incubation enjoy learning; they like designing experiments and carrying them out. [The people] in Acceleration ... have to love high-growth environments, where they solve a problem a minute ...

The first-level opportunity generators ... are lovers of information. They want to absorb and learn everything. They've also got the cre-ative side and are able to put disparate pieces of information together and articulate new opportunity spaces. This isn't done sitting at their desk; they absorb information everywhere. They're out and about and very creative in terms of the way they learn and who they talk to. Even in their desk research, they really go down into rat holes of learning that might be a little obtuse to others, and they're able to put the information together in very interesting ways ...

[The project level people in the Incubation phase], those doing the work, are good at two things. They are able to figure out what the next critical experiment should be, and they can figure out a disciplined way to design the experiment and run it. They have a discipline about them and can chart a course through the fog. They are executing, in our lexicon, the Learning Plan.

Acceleration includes all the experiments associated with moving a business opportunity to something more predictable so that you can decide whether to invest more heavily. At this stage, you're building the team; you're putting all the functions in place; you're identifying who the general manager of the business will be and who the head of marketing and operations will be. You're focused on manufacturing process innovation and finding operating efficiencies. What you're trying to do in Acceleration is show growth and a path towards profitability; you want to demonstrate that as the thing scales, you'll be making money.

At the top of [the Acceleration column in the matrix], we do not see a person, but instead a sort of governance committee, or Innovation Council. It's a shared responsibility, because when it's time for a new business initiative to be accelerated, that's where the big money commitments come in.

The businesses in [the Acceleration phase] are each led by a general manager for the new business ... Acceleration is where crises tend to occur, and you have to solve them quickly. By this time, you will have tested everything, but not at scale. These guys are problem solvers in crisis situations. But there are people who love that. They love the intensity, they love the urgency, they love the chaos, because there's such great excitement in the growth.

When a company is in the early stages of developing its management system, they don't need all nine roles. You sort of build up the function as you need it. But you need the concepts of discovery and incubation and acceleration, and you need to be thinking about them at the project, the platform, and the portfolio levels.

# 5

## Working with the Performance Engine: Graduated Engagement

### THE PROBLEM: WHERE YOU STAND DEPENDS ON WHERE YOU SIT

The Innovation Stage-Gate is concerned with innovation *capability*. It is focused on creating an innovation engine that is productive and that fits in the corporate setting.

The next challenge is to manage the *dynamics* of innovation in the corporate setting, which often means dealing with organizational resistance. Resistance to innovation is so prevalent in large companies that it is almost a proverb. It cuts across functions and across hierarchical levels and is a major reason that so many innovation programs do not achieve the business success that they could.

Dealing with resistance to innovation starts with the observation that resistance—though frustrating—is not irrational. People in organizations behave as you yourself would behave if you were in their shoes. Consciously or not, they calculate the best response to an innovation initiative—for their organization and for their own careers—and they act on that calculation. For those in the core functions, deviating from standard procedures is risky, at both a personal and a functional level. It is safer to stick to established ways of doing things. That the response is counterproductive to innovation is a side effect, not the objective.

Innovation teams often fail to appreciate this perspective. Instead, they tend to view those in the corporate functions as recalcitrant, reactionary, and unduly risk averse. As a result, they become angry, frustrated, and disempowered. They dig in their heels or escalate the lack of cooperation to higher management.

DOI: 10.4324/9780429433887-5

These are unproductive responses. They do not take into account that the people in the company's core functions have legitimate concerns. If the innovation team does not understand these concerns, and does not actively seek to manage the interaction between the venture and the core company, the innovation program can be slowed, or even smothered to the point of suffocation.

A few examples illustrate the point.

## Contracts 101

Imagine yourself as a bright, forward-looking contracts attorney inside a corporation.

One day, you are given a contract to review that is very different from a typical contract: It is focused on guaranteed service outcomes, rather than the sale of product. This is a new area for you. You don't really know what new risks might be involved or how to protect against them. You can see a few of the risks right off the bat, but you wonder what you might be missing. It is a small contract, so the downside may be limited, but the contract certainly isn't going to move the needle for the corporation in the next six months either. You know that the innovation team is hot to get this signed, but you think that perhaps you should do a little research first. You don't have the time just now, given that large product agreement that just came across your desk from the head of the division—a contract that needs to be signed before the end of the quarter. You will help, but only after you have done your research. The new venture contract goes to the bottom of the stack.

## The "Other" Category in Procurement

Something similar is happening in Procurement. The director of that function is considering a request from the innovation team for a new tracking system. She is asking herself, "What is this device, and what does it have to do with our business?" It doesn't fit in any of the standard procurement categories, so she is not sure why it has landed on her desk. Not a problem, really; she can identify alternative suppliers, qualify them, and get the selected vendors put on the approved vendor list. Then she can put out a Request for Proposal (RFP) and bid the thing out. The only problem is that there really *aren't* several vendors. If there were, she doesn't know what expertise would be required to qualify them, and her team is busy (as usual). The deal itself is for less than ten thousand dollars, hardly worth a big effort. Still, if the new venture ever goes forward, the company may buy millions of them. Better to negotiate now rather than wait for the pilot to end when her company might be locked into a supplier with no leverage. On top of these issues, the director is concerned that the vendor doesn't have the company's standard liability insurance coverage, and the company is so small that it doesn't seem capable of getting it. She can just imagine the liability risk. She sets up a meeting with her team to discuss alternate suppliers, but the innovation team wants to make the purchase now. The director longs for another straightforward purchase of 100 tons of carbon black!

You get the picture. Each department has analogous concerns and similar pressures. For these departments, the innovation team's requests come with little upside and a lot of (potential) downside (see Figure 5.1). No one says this out loud, of course, because innovation is a priority.

Back at the innovation department, people are pulling out their hair. Moving the new venture even a small step closer to reality seems to take Herculean effort. No one really says no, but everything drags out forever. Rapid iteration is not even possible. The tension builds. There has to be a better way.

## THE ROOT CAUSES OF RESISTANCE

Govindarajan and Trimble have coined a term for the functions that appear to resist innovation—the "performance engine." [Govindarajan and Trimble, 2010] The performance engine exists to maintain effective, efficient, and continuously improving operations—*not* to drive innovation. Innovation disrupts the performance engine and makes it harder for the people in the functions to keep the core business running. There is therefore an inherent conflict between the innovation team and the performance engine. This is what results in the appearance of resistance to innovation initiatives.

Lean Startup exacerbates this conflict in two general ways—through *disruption of work* and through the *undermining of standards*. Business experiments disrupt the work of the functions, yet they are the lifeblood of the Lean Startup method. They require people to set aside standard operating approaches and do things differently, at least for this project. Supporting innovation in this way can be risky for the people who work in the core for several reasons. First, it is easier to make mistakes in unfamiliar areas. Second, supporting a new venture may cause the function to shortchange its commitments to the core business client, a cardinal sin for a support group. Finally, supporting an innovation initiative may come at the risk of defying a supervising manager who is opposed to the initiative. Each of these risks is real to individuals in the functions, and they need to be acknowledged by innovation teams.

The second way that Lean Startup exacerbates the conflict is by undermining standards. For people who are leading functions—especially first-line managers—supporting innovation may mean making exceptions to the function's established standards. This can be hard for the function to accept. The innovation team may want to bypass the existing Stage-Gate™ product development process, for example, or it may need to use non-standard technologies (or even technologies for which the company does not yet have a standard operating environment). Standard practices for managing intellectual property or procurement may need to be relaxed to speed experimentation with clients or customers.

For the core functions, exceptions feel like a slippery slope. The processes and standards that they worked so hard to establish and to communicate and enforce will be undermined. The standards may not make sense for a new venture, but the functions fear that relaxing them will open a Pandora's box of exceptions. Any resulting erosion of standards will increase day-to-day costs for the function and raise the specter of future cost increases as the functions struggle to support non-standard products.

Both of these risks—to the individuals within the functions and to the standards that are essential to routine operations—need to be recognized and managed if a venture is to succeed in a corporate context. The good news is that this is possible. It starts with an innovation team understanding (and even honoring) the roles of those in the performance engine. Once the interests of the functions are well understood, they can be harmonized with the work of innovation.

## THE ROLE OF GAME THEORY

Making a collaboration between the functions and the innovation team work requires understanding the underlying dynamics of the organizational games being played. There is a branch of mathematics that can be used to do just that: Game theory. Game theory can help to identify and explain people's personal "payoff matrices"—the calculations that drive them to behave as they do. Once you understand these forces, you can make changes that shift the rules of the game in subtle but productive ways [Ritti and Funkhouser, 1977].

Game theory uses mathematical techniques to predict the behavior of actors in a social context. The underlying assumption is that people will, subconsciously or consciously, calculate their risk/reward (payoff) from any situation (game). It predicts that rational participants will act in a way that will *minimize their maximum loss*. Both of the general patterns of resistance to innovation can be explained with game theory and this heuristic for decision-making.

Many different types of games have been articulated and modeled by systems modelers. Each has its own payoff matrix and dynamics. Two of these games are important for internal innovators: The *Samaritan game* and the *Watchdog game*.

## The Samaritan Game

The first of the innovation games is the Good Samaritan game. It comes into play for those executing Lean Learning Loops in the corporate context.

Think of people in the functions as Samaritans, analogous to the Samaritan in the parable who helped the man who was robbed and left for dead. Like the Good Samaritan, those in the functions can choose to help the innovation function, likely for little reward, or they can choose to not help the innovation function, at some personal risk.

Choosing to help might come with a range of risks. It could put the person behind on other obligations or add to his workload. If the request is novel (as it often is), the person may make a mistake, and that mistake could have future consequences, which are at present unknown. On the other hand, the consequences of not helping are often minimal. The refusal may be explicit (an outright refusal to play) or implicit (repeated deferral of the request). In either case, the innovation team does not get the help it needs; it is, in fact, hampered by the expectation that it will.

Of course, helping the innovation team may offer some reward, but those rewards are mainly intrinsic, while negative consequences may affect the person's career path or bonus. As a result, there are few Good Samaritans, beyond those acting on the goodwill of existing relationships.

**TABLE 5.1**

The Function's Payoff Matrix for a Good Samaritan

|  | Innovation result | |
|---|---|---|
|  | **Something goes wrong** | **Everything goes well** |
| Function helps | Bonus affected | Atta boy |
| Function refuses to help | Mild admonition | Nothing |

For the function, the Good Samaritan payoff matrix looks like Table 5.1. As the table illustrates, the best solution for the core functions – the one that minimizes the maximum loss – is to refuse to help.

What can the innovation team do about this situation? An obvious choice—one often pursued with short-term benefit—is to raise the costs of noncompliance, for instance, by escalating the issue. Raising the costs of refusing to help can tip the payoff matrix, creating an incentive to help (or at least appear to be helping). But escalations quickly wear thin, for everyone involved, and they leave a trail of ill will.

Another tactic is to reduce the costs to the function of helping. Senior executives, for example, might provide air cover (clear permission), reducing the risk of a negative payout. Alternately, the innovation team might fund dedicated resources in the functions to support the innovation team, reducing the risk of the function not meeting its other obligations. Or the innovation team might explicitly accept part of the risk of any mistakes that may be made, perhaps by signing off on exceptions to normal practice.

This approach has the advantage of being sustainable. In many ways, it creates a win-win scenario. The people in the function get permission, resources, and the potential to use their capabilities in a new area. The innovation team gets the help that it would otherwise need to source from outside the company.

## The Watchdog Game

The second kind of innovation game is the Watchdog game. It comes into play for those building MVPs in the corporate context.

Part of the role of the manager of a function is to protect the function's territory and processes, like a watchdog protects its territory. What the manager is protecting is the standards and ways of doing things that the function has established over time. The rules can seem bureaucratic and inappropriate to innovation teams, but they are there for a reason. The functions that have the strongest watchdog character are usually product development and IT; they have the most to lose if things get out of control because—inevitably—they will be accountable for permitting the project to move forward.

Confronted with a request from the innovation team, watchdogs have a choice: They can permit exceptions to policy to help the innovation function or they can stick to their guns. Often, they choose to stick to their guns, primarily out of a fear that one exception will lead to another, and pretty soon, the world they manage will become unmanageably chaotic. The costs of dealing with the exceptions will overwhelm the function and reduce the quality of their output. The watchdog sees how an apparently innocuous exception could have negative long-term consequences.

Again, it's not hard for the function to undermine what the innovation team is trying to do. They can refuse resources to those who do not follow the established process or who do not work with the standard operating environment. They can demand a study of the proposed exception, which may take a very long time. They can escalate the innovation team's noncompliance, which can result in cycles of meetings and justifications. Whatever the function does, the innovation team does not get the permission or the resources that it needs to proceed. The project is needlessly delayed.

Of course, the watchdog may also see some reward in helping the innovation team succeed. For instance, the innovation team may be on the cutting edge of a new trend that will affect the function in the future, like open-source software, cloud computing, or agile development. But most of these megatrends fade or are so delayed that they present more of a risk than an opportunity for the function.

On the other hand, if something is going to go wrong, it's likely to happen much sooner than any trend will come to fruition. And as soon as it does, the manager will likely be called to task: Why did he or she permit this to happen? Don't they understand the importance of standards? For the functional manager, the negative consequences of appearing to lose control of the function may far outweigh the risk of not being on the cutting edge of new technologies or practices. As a result, watchdogs tread very carefully.

The watchdog's payoff matrix looks like Table 5.2.

Permitting an exception comes with the biggest downside to the function. If something goes wrong—the solution fails, the product is hard

**TABLE 5.2**

Payoff Matrix for the Watchdog

|  | Innovation result | |
|---|---|---|
|  | **Something goes wrong** | **Everything goes well** |
| Function permits exceptions to support innovation | Manager called to the task; budget issues | Atta boy |
| Function refuses to permit exceptions | Mild rebuke | Nothing |

to maintain, or costs are high—the manager is held to account for letting it happen. Clearly, the best choice for the watchdog manager is to drag his or her feet or at least to scrutinize the new request carefully before allowing it.

What can the innovation team do about this? The biggest concern of a watchdog is that any exception will get out of control: An experiment that starts small will turn into a deployed system that has to be maintained; everyone will want an exception, and the costs of managing the function will skyrocket; the alternative may not even work, and the functional lead will be held accountable—even though he or she objected up front.

The innovation team can help to reduce these concerns, through a process I call "graduated engagement" (see Figure 5.1). The basis for graduated engagement is the Innovation Stage-Gate. The idea is that the

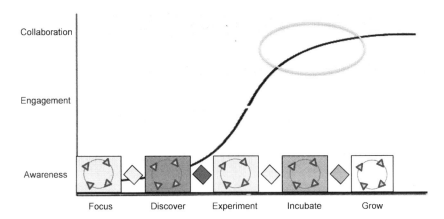

**FIGURE 5.1**

Graduated engagement

innovation team engages with the function with increasing intensity as the project progresses through the stages of the Innovation Stage-Gate. At the earliest stages, the functions are made aware of what is happening; they can ask questions but cannot impose standards or processes. Everything is too provisional and exploratory for it to matter.

At Incubation, a new phase is triggered. During that stage, which may last for several months or even a year, the innovation team works with the functions to define what it will take to scale the initiative. Standard operating environments are considered at this point—and created if they do not yet exist for a technology. During this phase, any needed product or system is redeveloped in a way that the core function can support and that satisfies core requirements for scalability, security, and maintainability. Issues with liability or accounting or intellectual property are thoroughly addressed.

Two things make this approach work. First, graduated engagement creates a clear point at which critical functions can make sure their concerns are addressed. This engagement happens, however, without slowing the innovation process. Second, the visibility that it provides reduces free-floating anxiety about hypothetical future problems. The early stages also give the innovation team and the functions the chance to identify and begin to address potential issues early. The lack of time pressure lowers the temperature and lets the issues be dealt with more rationally. Graduated engagement is a more sustainable practice than escalation and one that encourages collaboration, not conflict.

---

## SUMMARY: MANAGING RESISTANCE TO INNOVATION

There is a saying: Where you stand depends on where you sit. In other words, the way you view a particular issue depends on the role you play in the company. This is certainly true for a company's functional leaders. This insight is at the heart of game theory, which assumes that each party will act according to his or her personal assessment of the payoff matrix. What the payoff matrix looks like depends on where you sit in the company.

To change behavior, you need to shift the payoff matrix for key players in the organizational games that are always going on. How you shift a given individual's payoff matrix depends on the issue and the game being played. In the Samaritan game, the personal risks associated with helping the innovation team can be reduced with air cover and with dedicated resources to support the innovation effort. Watchdog games, which revolve around the organizational risks functions face in helping the innovation team, can be managed via graduated engagement and risk-sharing.

Suggestions for managing the inherent conflict with corporate functions are covered in a paper that Abhijit Ganguly and I wrote on "Conducting Business Experiments." An excerpt of that paper is included in this chapter.

## CONDUCTING BUSINESS EXPERIMENTS

### ABHIJIT GANGULY AND JIM EUCHNER

Govindarajan and Trimble (2010) discuss the inherent conflicts between any innovation initiative and what they call the company's "performance engine." These conflicts arise frequently in the context of business experiments, as experiments can challenge the working practices of existing functions and at times require exceptions to those practices. The specifics of the conflicts will vary by industry and cultural factors, but there are patterns. The most common conflicts concern intellectual property, marketing, risk management, procurement, and sales.

**Intellectual Property.** A strong intellectual property regime can be a key element of competitive advantage, and business experiments often come with the risk of exposing elements of intellectual property related to the concepts being tested. In many companies, concern about even limited exposure of an idea before patent applications are filed drives strict policies regarding disclosure. Goodyear protects intellectual property in business experiments but takes a different approach than that of the core business. Customers participating in experiments are informed that the information they will see is confidential and are asked to agree to keep it confidential. In some cases, that agreement is a simple, one-page form; in others, it is a verbal communication. In a few cases, when the concept seemed likely to result in a patentable invention, we have filed provisional patents before sharing it. We have not had any intellectual property issues arising from business experiments.

**Marketing.** Companies spend significant resources and time developing their brands. On occasion, concerns may arise that an experiment could damage the brand image with a particular customer set or some other stakeholder. Often, this concern can be avoided by not using the brand or logo in the experiment. When the brand is central to the experiment—when we believe that the success of the endeavor depends on its being offered by Goodyear—we work closely with the marketing function in designing the experiment. If the experiment is conducted in a local test market for a limited period of time, and if the marketing function has the chance to review the materials ahead of the experiment, it is often (but not always) possible to move forward with the experiment.

**Risk Management.** There is the potential in any experiment for something to go wrong, whether through a failure of the technology or a failure of the concept. It is possible that the failure might result in consequential damages. The need to manage liability can therefore be an impediment to conducting certain experiments. However, at times there is no way to learn about a new concept without conducting a real-world experiment, with all of its attendant risks. When we do such an experiment, we seek to identify the risks before the experiment begins, mitigate them as much as possible, note any concerns that can't be fully mitigated, and document how they will be handled if they arise. We engage in practices analogous to those we use when conducting trials of new products in the core business. Careful experimental design, together with open discussion of possible risks with participating customers, is critical.

**Procurement.** We often conduct experiments with technology developed by partners. These experiments are generally designed to provide an opportunity to learn about the technology's potential to support a new business. These experiments come with a risk that the collaboration could compromise future negotiations with that partner in some way. At Goodyear, we have mitigated the risk of ill feeling or compromised negotiating position by creating different types of agreements for different stages of business building. At the early stages, we may experiment with an off-the-shelf offering. If the partner is a startup or a small enterprise, we may enter into a joint development arrangement to pilot the technology, with intellectual property terms defined but business terms to be determined. In other instances, business negotiations may be deferred until we are clear about the business potential and can negotiate with clear intent. This flexibility works to the benefit of both parties; without it, the experiments can be significantly delayed.

**Sales.** Because business model innovation is aimed at creating growth in areas adjacent to the core business, we often work with customers of the company's performance engine. This can create issues with the sales organization for two reasons. First, anything that is not a sale of a core product can be a distraction to the sales force, which already must meet challenging targets. Second, the sales organization may not agree with the concept being tested and may not want to expose it to customers. Sales organizations also have a natural concern that the innovation function may appear to promise something that may never be brought to market, and by doing so, may disappoint the customer. When approaching customers, we work with the sales organizations; we spend time discussing the concept and the experiment design with sales management. Often, we get useful feedback on the concepts. We also get good insight into which customers might be the right first targets. Done well, these discussions result in better experiments. Early in the business model innovation process, sales personnel will often accompany the innovation team in meetings with customers; over time, as trust builds, access to customers typically becomes more open.

Business experiments present clear risks in each of these areas, but there are also risks in *not* conducting experiments. Principal among these is that you will build the wrong product or service, partner with the wrong partner, or go to market with the wrong business model. Furthermore, the learning from these experiments, and from customers in particular, is very powerful in building internal support for the business you are building. Conducting experiments—even "quick" experiments—can take time, but they can help the organization to understand the opportunity and ultimately lead to a stronger offering.

## KEY INSIGHTS

- Business experiments are an essential way of reducing the risks of a new business and are at the heart of the Lean Startup
- Conducting business experiments in the context of the performance engine can be challenging, especially when they require putting products (or MVPs) into the hands of users
- Game theory can be used to design approaches that increase internal collaboration and permit the experiments to proceed
- The most important practices for working with the performance engine are Air Cover, Risk-Sharing, and Graduated Engagement.

# 6

## Achieving Strategic Alignment: Asset-Based Opportunity Spaces

### WHY US?

A startup is not a smaller version of a large corporation; neither is a new business inside a corporation just a startup that happens to be hosted by a large company. For a new venture to be successful inside the corporate context, it must align with the strategic directions of the hosting company. Often, these strategic directions are not clearly stated. Discovering the boundaries of the company's strategy and building ventures that can leverage the assets of the corporation is critical. Unfortunately, misalignments are often discovered too late in the process, to the disappointment of both executives and innovation teams.

The underlying cause of the frustration is a failure to set meaningful boundaries. Defining opportunity spaces helps. They provide the innovation team with guardrails that keep the team from straying too far from corporate strategy. If the company uses an Innovation Stage-Gate, opportunity spaces provide the basis for a strategic review of an initiative. One question the innovation team should answer is, "Why us?"

As noted above, Vijay Govindarajan estimates that, to succeed, an internal venture should leverage about 40% of its critical assets from the hosting company. These may be the customer base, core technologies, brand permission, or the service infrastructure, for example. The careful repurposing of an existing asset—if managed well—can provide significant advantages to the new company. Failure to do so begs the question, "Why us? Why do we think that we will be more successful with this venture than a startup, with its speed and flexibility, would be?"

DOI: 10.4324/9780429433887-6

## ASSET-BASED OPPORTUNITY SPACES

An opportunity space is an area that is ripe for innovation. It may result from a new technology (or combination of technologies), from demographic shifts, from changes in customer behaviors, from new regulations, or from some combination of these. The major trends in the automotive industry, for example, are autonomy (driven by rapid advances in sensors and AI technology); electrification (supported to a large degree by environmental regulations and subsidies); shared use of transportation (which is driving new patterns in ownership and the emergence of consumer fleets); and connectivity (which is enabling new consumer use cases for the time customers spend in a vehicle). These trends are driving billions of dollars in investment, spawning hundreds of startups, and blurring longstanding industry boundaries. There are more opportunities in this space than there have been for years.

The opportunity space, however, will differ for each company. What creates the opportunity space is the *intersection* between the trends and the assets of an ongoing business. In the insurance industry, for example, the opportunity may be in the use of information technology and autonomy to significantly reduce casualty losses. A new partnership between insurance companies and automotive companies may make sense to both. In the logistics industry, the trends might enable new forms of collaborative shipping or new ways to reduce costs through driver-assist and route optimization. In the tire industry, the opportunity might be in support of consumer fleets, leveraging experience learned in commercial trucking.

Defining the opportunity spaces takes time. Many people can see trends; few are adept at repurposing assets.

A company can leverage many assets to grow into new markets. The six most common assets that can be leveraged are (see Figure 6.1):

- *Customer base*: The customer base for one product may overlap with the customer base for another product, even one that seems quite different. A corner gas station today, for example, sells food, coffee, lottery tickets, firewood, and propane.
- *Channel*: An established channel can be used to push a very different set of products. For instance, Frito-Lay leveraged its supermarket channel to sell cookies in addition to salty snacks.

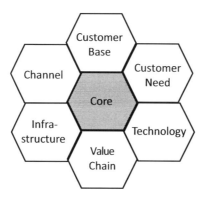

**FIGURE 6.1**
Leveraging assets to move into new markets

- *Infrastructure*: The infrastructure for one business may support a very different business. Williams Pipeline, which repurposed its unused network of gas pipelines to carry fiber-optic cable for long-haul telecommunications, for example
- *Value chain*: Companies can move upstream or downstream in their value chain. It was popular in the industrial age for companies to be vertically integrated, in industries from steel to automobiles
- *Technology*: Technical expertise can be applied in new markets. For instance, Ball Corporation (the Mason jar company) has applied its expertise in container technologies in a wide variety of industries, from foods to aerospace
- *Underlying customer need*: A company that understands its customers' needs deeply can migrate with the customer into new ways of meeting that need. Netflix's move from movies on CD to streaming and content development is such an example—though they were ahead of many customers in anticipating their preference for streaming.

Leveraging assets to move into new businesses is a double-edged sword. On the one hand, it greatly increases an internal venture's chance of success. On the other hand, repurposing an asset that is part of the smoothly operating machine that is the core business—the performance engine—can be very disruptive.

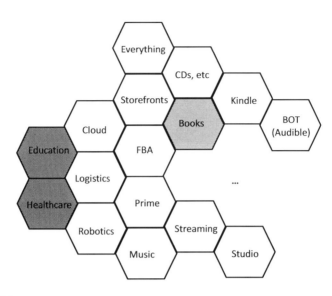

**FIGURE 6.2**
Amazon.com adjacencies

The process of identifying asset-based opportunity spaces is idiosyncratic. It can start with a market opportunity and seek to identify ways of developing competitive advantage by leveraging or extending existing assets. The categories listed above are fruitful hunting grounds. Alternately, innovators can start with existing assets and envision new or extended uses for them. This can be especially powerful when a company is able to leverage assets from different parts of the corporation in a synergistic way. Finally, at times, if you are alert to it, the market will point to opportunities to use existing assets in new ways. Customers may see something that you don't.

Amazon is a master at innovation that leverages assets developed for one business to move into another. It has made such moves multiple times, converting internal assets into the building blocks for new businesses. Figure 6.2 is a partial map of how they have done this.

- *Customer base*: Amazon moved from selling books to selling CDs, toys, and many other items, leveraging and strengthening its customer base
- *Channel*: Amazon opened up its channel to competitors with its Marketplaces offering, which provides access to Amazon's customer base and its web infrastructure through Amazon Storefronts. This move included presenting competitor products

on an equal footing to those sold directly by Amazon, including pricing transparency. The decision to open up its channel was very controversial both inside Amazon and on Wall Street—it was viewed as literally "giving away the store"—but Marketplaces enabled Amazon to sell a much wider variety of things (see Brad Stone's book, *The Everything Store*) [Stone, 2013]

- *Infrastructure*: Amazon developed expertise in warehousing and logistics to support its own growing business. It now provides these services to affiliated sellers through Fulfillment by Amazon (FBA). Amazon Prime, which provides free shipping for Amazon products, has been extended in some cases to affiliates. Amazon's scale as a logistics company is now comparable to that of the United Parcel Service (UPS) and Federal Express

- *Value chain*: Amazon leveraged its Prime subscription offering, which initially provided free shipping for e-tail customers, to move into streaming music and then video. The company began by streaming other producers' offerings and then moved upstream in the value chain for video, becoming an independent film studio

- *Technology*: Amazon developed for its own use a very strong infrastructure for cloud computing. Early in its evolution, it began to sell this asset to third parties as elastic storage and elastic computing capabilities. It is now the leading provider of cloud computing services, which account for a major portion of its revenues. Again, there was significant internal resistance to opening up the "crown jewels" to the world

- *Underlying customer needs*: As customers shifted some of their reading from paper to electronic forms, Amazon entered the e-book business with its Kindle device, the Kindle app, and the Kindle store. The Kindle product and its supporting assets have led to a shift from physical to electronic books for many readers. It also purchased audible.com, which now bundles audiobooks with some Kindle purchases.

Amazon continues to grow into new businesses that leverage its assets. It has moved into Amazon Care, originally provided only to Amazon employees in Washington State. Amazon describes Amazon Care on its website:

> *Amazon Care has two components: 1) virtual care, which connects patients to medical professionals via the Amazon Care app … and allows patients to quickly, conveniently, and confidently chat live with a nurse or doctor, via in-app messaging or video; and 2) in-person care, where Amazon Care can dispatch a medical professional to a patient's home for additional care, ranging from routine blood draws to listening to a patient's lungs, and also offer prescription delivery right to a patient's door.*

Amazon announced a national rollout of this service, including to non-employees, for the summer of 2021. The asset it leveraged in this case was its own employee base.

Amazon has also recently launched Machine Learning University, which will use Amazon scientists to offer online training and credentials in artificial intelligence. This capability will help to identify and train its future workforce and could compete with branded universities in its space.

Many of these asset-based innovation initiatives leverage a combination of assets (customer base and channel or value chain and technology, for example). The key is that, in each case, core assets provide an impressive source of competitive advantage; redeploying assets creatively has enabled the company to win in market after market.

As noted above, leveraging assets to create new businesses is difficult. Often, there is resistance to ceding a competitive advantage in the core business (and even helping to create new competitors). At other times, there is a concern that the new business will distract from and disrupt the core. Amazon confronted these challenges and used some of the tools discussed later in this book, including organizing for growth and developing ambidextrous leaders.

Although sharing assets of the core business with an internal startup can be difficult, it is also difficult for large companies to win in a new market without leveraging assets. A large company typically needs the advantages conferred by these assets to overcome the disadvantages of its size.

---

## JOHN ROSSMAN ON *INNOVATION THE AMAZON WAY*

John Rossman created the Marketplaces business at Amazon and has reflected in depth on what makes Amazon so successful. This chapter includes an excerpt from an extensive interview with Rossman, titled "Innovation the Amazon Way." Rossman illustrates asset-based innovation [Rossman and Euchner, 2108] from the perspective of a master practitioner.

## INNOVATION THE AMAZON WAY

## AN INTERVIEW WITH JOHN ROSSMAN

Customer obsession is everybody's job at Amazon. Everybody is expected to understand the customer deeply. You need to understand customers, not just at the narrow intersection at which you happen to be dealing with them, but in a broader sense, as well. You're expected to be able to use data to substantiate your position about the customer. Wherever possible, you also want to be a customer yourself, so you're working to develop empathy. You look for lots of ways to get critical, demanding feedback from customers. You don't look for the happy stories; you look for the dissatisfied, quiet, hidden stories from your customers.

And you're willing to do hard things. You're willing to invent and improve and pursue new opportunities that are not easy or obvious. As Bezos says, "You have to be willing to be misunderstood," often for a long period of time ...

Innovation happens in a lot of different ways, and there's no one right way to do it. There is what I would call "small i" innovation and "big I" innovation. The "small i" innovation is the innovation and the improvements that come from asking, "How do we take what we're doing today and do it better? How do we do it perfectly?" That work is always around your classical operational improvement objectives of decreasing defects, improving quality issues, decreasing costs, reducing safety issues, and increasing your throughput.

Many of Amazon's innovations start with, How do we do what we're doing today perfectly? Whether that is to fulfill an order or to avoid a customer contact or to provide the availability and speed that's required in the AWS [Amazon Web Services] business, it doesn't matter. It's about being relentless. If you go to relentless.com, that leads you to Amazon. The company is relentless in its pursuit of perfection.

The "big I" innovation at Amazon is centered around the notion of being a platform company. A platform company is a company that takes a core capability and makes it good enough to serve not just itself, but external clients as well. Part of the benefit of serving external clients is that they are much more demanding than internal clients. Forcing yourself to have external clients can not only create a good business if done correctly, but it also makes your service better for your own organization to use. That's where Amazon Web Services came from, and that's where FBA [Fulfillment by Amazon] came from. Both derive from the same notion.

Amazon also uses the metaphor of a flywheel for its business strategy. It's about creating momentum in your business and pursuing the long-term assets that your customers will always treasure—to create them and to always be building on them. I remember hearing Bezos talk about how he can't imagine a world where customers would want to pay more or have less selection or slower delivery. So, one of the things Amazon has always done is to pursue competitive pricing, more selection, and faster delivery to customers. While the company goes about those things at times in incremental ways, it is making long-term investments; they are pursuits that the company has been committed to for a long period of time. Being centered on those long-term customer needs and core corporate assets has helped center Amazon's investments in innovation ...

AWS [Amazon Web Services] didn't start out as a big bet. It started back in 2003 or 2004 as a question: How do we create a better and more scalable infrastructure for our own needs? A little later we thought, "Let's make this better and see if external developers would like it." We were forcing the infrastructure team to have external clients and to drive toward self-service for those clients. And what we found was that developers loved that self-service, on-demand infrastructure. So, the company started pursuing that business, and over time, it has put more and more and more commitment into it. But it didn't start off as a massive commitment. It started with a big idea, a big vision, but with incremental steps and trials to realize the vision.

Relative to managing the internal tension, one of the things Amazon talks about is that platform businesses need to be self-service. People who want to use your capability shouldn't have to talk to you in order to use it. The platform needs to abstract the complexity; it needs to be obvious in its use; it needs to be predictive in its management requirements; and it needs to be self-service. So much of Amazon's scale and innovation has come from the notion of making things self-service. The way we scaled the Marketplace business was by taking a very complex integration and working in lots of ways to make it self-service. We wanted to develop the business so that a seller wouldn't have to talk with us in order to start selling on Amazon. Similarly, a developer doesn't need to talk to somebody at Amazon to start using AWS. Forcing things to be self-service forces you to make them simpler, and that's why invent *and* simplify is the principle, not just invent. Simplification is part of the core value proposition of many platform businesses at Amazon ...

[Whether to set up a separate business or not for an innovation] completely depends on the situation. There's no tripping wire or specific threshold. In the case of Marketplace, we separated the Marketplace team from retail initially but coordinated thoroughly. It was a much smaller organization back in 2002 and 2003, and we separated it from the retail team because at Marketplace we were building competition for the Amazon retail team. We didn't want to bury our very small organization deep within retail because we wanted a separation to create competition. Once we were successful, however, we reintegrated back into the retail business. It really depends on the situation whether you start out integrated or separated and whether, at some point, you reintegrate or you stay separate ...

[W]hen we were launching this in 2002, it wasn't clear that we were going to win. eBay was the dominant marketplace business. Amazon had tried a couple of versions as a third-party selling business that hadn't been successful. We were taking the third run at it, and it wasn't clear we were going to be successful. In fact, it took a long time for it to build to success; it took a couple of additional pieces to drive that success, including the development of Prime as a customer loyalty program and the development of FBA [Fulfillment by Amazon]. It was the combination of the Marketplace platform with Prime and FBA that created the dramatic growth in the third-party business at Amazon. And that was a few years after we launched the business, so Amazon was very patient with that business ...

Bezos is on record talking about the fact this quarter's results are based on things that were put in place months ago if not a year or two ago. The things you're doing now are impacting forward quarter results. The intuition and the experience to know the difference between the things that are in your control today versus the things that are not within your control today is critical. If you miss financial results, of course you're going to do a deep dive to understand why. But the focus is not typically on the things that you were doing recently; it is on the things you were doing a long time ago that led to the recent missed quarterly results …

Big operational leaders [at Amazon] typically have both operational things they're striving for and innovation goals. It depends on the situation. I mentioned earlier work in supply chain. There's a lot of operational execution going on there at Amazon, as well as a lot of innovation. Senior leadership at Amazon deals in both of those worlds, and they bring the ideas and their execution together in lots of different ways …

[B]usiness model innovations require bucking up against the traditions of the industry. They are the essence of a lot of great innovation, but they are the hardest kind of innovation for companies to do. Almost inevitably, they are going to upset the apple cart. They're going to upset partners, they're going to upset suppliers, and they are also going to upset some internal employees, like the sales force. When you truly want to innovate your business model, you need to "be willing to be misunderstood for a long period of time," as Bezos says. But the results can be remarkable.

## KEY INSIGHTS

- A new venture inside a corporation needs a "right to win" against more nimble startups
- Asset-based opportunity spaces—which leverage corporate assets to move into growth markets—can provide both focus and sources of competitive advantage
- There are six key types of assets that companies can leverage to move into new and adjacent spaces
- Leveraging core assets can be difficult; the core business will often resist, especially if leveraging the assets might cannibalize the core business
- Amazon is a master at asset-based innovation and at defining opportunity spaces that leverage core assets; much can be learned from studying their approach.

# 7

## Introducing a New Business Model: The Business Model Pyramid

### THE PROBLEM: BUSINESS MODEL INERTIA

There is a strong tendency for companies to bring a new venture to market using their existing business model or some variant of it. This can lead to a business model that is not well-suited to the new venture, and the mismatch can actually destroy value. Even when the default business model can be made to work, it very frequently leaves money on the table.

This impulse to default to the current business model has some good underlying reasons, which is why it is so common. First, the current business model has likely been optimized over many years and has a track record of delivering results—reliably, predictably, and at low cost. Why start from scratch? Second, constructing a new business model from scratch is risky. It may require developing new channels, new pricing models, and even new operating models. These take time, and mistakes are inevitable. Finally, elements of the new business model may disrupt the smooth operations of the core business, creating costs no firm wants to absorb.

These are legitimate concerns. But when a company locks onto its current business model and attempts to apply the same model to breakthrough innovations, it locks out business models that are likely to be much better.

Consider, as an example, the way that product companies have most often chosen to take their smart, connected product capabilities to market. Many manufacturers have invested heavily in the Internet of Things (IoT), adding sensors, creating cloud-based platforms for sharing data, developing intelligent algorithms for diagnosing customer problems, and creating web-based dashboards for presenting product data to users.

DOI: 10.4324/9780429433887-7

These components frequently create value that a company should be able to capture.

Product-centric companies with product-centric business models often seek to capture value by asking a premium price for the smart product or by creating an add-on subscription service. Alternately, IoT components are often sold as adjuncts to the product, and their success is measured by their impact on pull-through sales of the core product or on maintenance contract sales. Unfortunately, customers are often unwilling to pay extra for the "bells and whistles" because the technology doesn't, in and of itself, create value. As a result, the investment in IoT fails to capture its costs.

A shift in business model—from a product-centric to a services-led model—may enable the company both to create more value for customers and to capture more value for itself. In a services-led model, the company sells not the product but the use of the product or the business outcome the customer seeks. Digital technology, including IoT components, is a key enabler for improving the performance of the product in use from the customer's point of view. A services-led business model broadens the value proposition to include outcomes and enables the supplier to create—and capture—substantially greater customer value. Services-led business models have been successfully employed by a number of venerable manufacturers, among them Rolls-Royce, Caterpillar, The Goodyear Tire & Rubber Company, and Castrol.

But a services-led business model is very different from a product-centric business model:

- The product itself is conceptualized differently. Rather than an object—a physical product with digital add-ons—the company sells an outcome—improved uptime or increased throughput, for example
- Revenue is based not on product sales but on customer outcomes
- Measures of success shift from product sales to customer-focused metrics; the company's success is tied directly to the success of its customers according to their own criteria
- Design priorities change; the product may now be designed for increased life and ease of service, neither of which may be justifiable in a business model based on new product sales

- Customer relationships are reshaped. Contact with the customer is more frequent and is often focused not on the product itself but on customer outcomes and how they might be improved
- Spare parts supply chains receive closer attention. They may have to be reengineered to increase responsiveness and reduce downtime, since the supplier will now absorb more of the costs of downtime
- Contracting will evolve. Contracts may include clauses that impose liability on the manufacturer for outages or failures of the product.

In other words, implementing a services-led model—or any other model that is radically different from the company's dominant model—may require differences in *six or more elements of the business model.*

## WHAT IS A BUSINESS MODEL?

*A business model is the set of strategic choices a firm uses to create and sustain margins and to grow in a competitive environment.*

The elements of a business model can be represented using the Business Model Canvas, which is one of the most popular tools used for business model innovation today [Osterwalder and Euchner, 2019]. Although the canvas is effective in creating awareness and encouraging broad thinking about the possibilities for business model innovation, it does not capture the critical elements that make a business model successful in practice.

There are three attributes of a good business model that go beyond the Business Model Canvas. These attributes are systemic: They address the interrelatedness of the business model elements and their dynamics. The three elements are:

1. *Coherence*: The parts of the business model are designed to reinforce one another. Brainstorming of the elements of the business model is unlikely to create a coherent whole
2. *Competitive Advantage*: The business model creates points of important differentiation in the marketplace; for established companies, this is often the leveraging of an existing asset in a new way
3. *Economic Leverage*: The economics of the business model get better as the business scales.

None of the attributes above is captured on the Business Model Canvas (though there are currently attempts to augment the canvas to address some of the gaps).

## HOW DO YOU DO BUSINESS MODEL INNOVATION?

Business model innovation is difficult, but it need not be as fraught with risk as is often thought. It should be engaged in systematically and with an experimental mindset. New business models inside corporations fail for predictable reasons:

- The business tries to capture value before it has a clear view of the customer value created
- The new venture defaults to the current business model or to the one that most readily comes to mind
- The venture team fails to consider the full range of risks to the business early enough in the process
- The new venture team fails to consider fully the risks that the new business may create for the core, which leads to resistance when the business is ready to launch
- The venture team fails to do what it can to understand and manage business risks before going to market
- The business is launched without an incubation period, during which issues of profitability and scalability are addressed.

The Business Model Pyramid (Figure 7.1) deals with each of these points of failure in turn. It helps innovation teams move systematically from high uncertainty and high risk to lower uncertainty and lower risk. The Business Model Pyramid was developed at Goodyear Tire & Rubber Company, an established company with a very strong culture and an established business model, where it was used successfully to launch four new businesses on three continents [Euchner and Ganguly, 2014]. The elements of the model are:

1. Validation of customer value created
2. Active consideration of alternative business model archetypes
3. Identification and assessment of the risks of each model

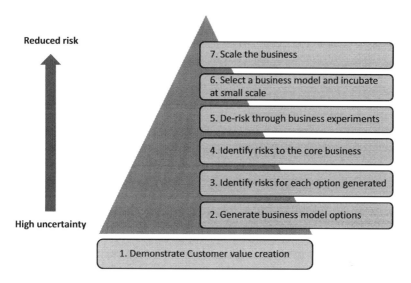

**Reduced risk**

7. Scale the business

6. Select a business model and incubate at small scale

5. De-risk through business experiments

4. Identify risks to the core business

3. Identify risks for each option generated

2. Generate business model options

**High uncertainty**

1. Demonstrate Customer value creation

**FIGURE 7.1**
The Business Model Pyramid

4. Modeling of the specific risks to the parent organization
5. Reducing risks through business experiments
6. Incubation of the business on a small scale.

Each of these is discussed below.

## 1. Start with a Clear Understanding of Customer Value

It is critical to understand the value your business concept will create for prospective customers. This value should be articulated in clear and quantitative terms as early in the process as possible. Without a clear understanding of customer value creation, the business model development is likely to be wishful rather than fact-based.

It is important to stress that you cannot *create* value with a new business model; a new business model can only help you to *capture* value. One can only create value by meeting a real customer need in a compelling way for a critical mass of people. This seems obvious, but innovation teams are easily diverted by concerns about capturing value before they understand how much value they might create. The strength of the value proposition creates the value; the strength of the business model lets you capture more or less of the value you create.

A compelling value proposition must create a lot more value than it costs to deliver to make it worth the effort of developing and testing a new business model. As noted above, business model innovation is fraught with risk, uncertainty, and internal resistance. If there is a big enough prize, you can make it work; if the prize is not so big, you are very likely to fail in creating the business.

It is important to attempt to quantify customer value. The first step is usually to identify categories of value, which may require interviews and observations of customers. The next step is to make estimates of the ranges of value likely created. These estimates force you to be concrete and provide a basis for further study. Finally, you need to validate this understanding with real customers, perhaps as part of a trial or through a business experiment.

A startup I worked with uses drones to design solar installations for residential and commercial buildings. The company is able to provide superior designs, account for insolation differences in their designs, develop parts lists that minimize waste, translate the data into CAD/CAM systems—and do so notably faster than manual methods, which increases customer acceptance rates. The company had not calculated the value they created for customers. When we did the math, we discovered that their business model—based on a subscription revenue model—was capturing 3% of the value created. A different business model, which made the value creation visible to the customer, permitted an increase in value capture of three to five times, depending on the segment.

## 2. Identify Business Model Options

A great business model hangs together. The parts reinforce one another and bring the concept to life. There is synergy in the true sense of the word. A good business model is often replicated across industries or sectors; over time, it becomes a proven archetype.

There is a limited number of effective business model archetypes. Adrian Slywotzky has identified 23 core models (see *The Art of Profitability*) and explored several others (see *How Digital Is Your Business?*). It is useful to become familiar with all of these core archetypes, even in a digital world. They provide a basis for understanding the piece parts and power of a truly good business model: What makes it work, what levers are critical to its success, and the sources of its profitability. The underlying dynamics are often subtle, so the learning curve takes time.

The digital age has spawned a Cambrian explosion of new business models, from hyper-targeted advertising, Direct-to-Consumer (D2C) businesses, and the shared economy to multi-sided platforms and predictive selling. Many of these models have emerged in several different industry contexts, and they are evolving and being optimized over time. It is valuable to seek to understand these models, their underlying dynamics, and where they are most applicable.

Archetypes are an excellent starting place for business model innovation. Developing a new business model in practice is usually a process of *structured selection*: A business model archetype is selected that might be an effective means of bringing a value proposition to market, and that model is adapted to the details of the new business.

A key element in the search for business model archetypes is to look for assets that you might be able to leverage in creating a new business based on your value proposition. If you are able to build a new business on a proven business model archetype and to do so in a way that leverages core assets, you can greatly increase the chances of success and reduce time to market.

For any radically new customer value proposition, it is useful to consider three or four business models. The first may be a variant of the current business model. The second may be one that is somewhat different from your current model but comes to mind very quickly. The third and fourth alternatives will require more thought and may open up possibilities that make a real difference.

To decide among the alternatives, you need to apply them to your situation. Understanding how a model might play out in your context requires effort and attention. I suggest approaching that effort sequentially, taking the same steps for each candidate model:

1. Map out the elements of the archetype and their application in the business you are building
2. Create a very high-level P&L for the proposed business; the assumptions may all be wrong, but the exercise will give you a clearer sense of the business model and the critical economics
3. If the model looks promising, try to identify companies that are using the business model archetype in a non-competing industry; if you

can, benchmark a few to understand how current practitioners think about capturing value with the model and to identify the underlying processes that make the model work

4. Get feedback on the business model from potential customers in your industry; test it as part of your value proposition.

Many companies gloss over the analysis of potential business models. Frequently, the business model decision is made by default. Even when the business team considers alternatives, it often doesn't really study them. This superficial approach makes it more likely that the team will lock onto a model that looks attractive and lock out alternatives—perhaps missing the real opportunity to create and capture value. Adrian Slywotzky discusses business designs and how to go about creating powerful, profitable businesses in an interview excerpted below [Slywotzky and Euchner, 2015].

## 3. Study Business Model Risks Broadly

It is easy to fall in love with a beautiful business model, but the model must be rigorously assessed. There is a natural tendency of innovators to focus on identifying and addressing only the execution risks associated with the business. But many ventures fail because they don't consider a wide enough range of what could go wrong. It is important to identify all critical risks early because some of them may be showstoppers.

Ron Adner has developed an approach for uncovering these risks. He calls his approach the Wide Lens [Adner, 2013]. Adner makes the point that many innovators focus their efforts primarily on reducing the risks that they understand the best—those related to execution— not on those that they understand the least. Execution risks are often managed with great care while other risks are ignored.

Adner has identified two other categories of risk: *Co-innovation risks* and *adoption chain risks*. Co-innovation risks relate to innovation that must be successfully executed by others. Such risks are increasingly prevalent in a world that relies on ecosystems for success. Ecosystem partners may or may not deliver in a timely way the critical elements necessary for the success of your new value proposition.

As development partnerships have become more common, successful companies have become increasingly adept at the management of co-innovation risks. This is true even though there are frequently issues on both sides of joint projects that impede progress. The most common of these are IP concerns, negotiation of eventual commercial terms, and arms-length development practices that assume that all of the technical challenges have been defined by requirements documents.

Adoption chain risks, Adner's second category of risks, arise when others in the value chain to the customer decide not to cooperate in making your innovation successful. An adoption chain partner may be part of your business model's distribution, sales, service, or supply chain. It might be a regulator or a platform provider. Anything new that is required of an adoption chain partner must be worthwhile to that partner, both economically and strategically, if you are to gain their support for your venture. If your business model design does not care for these parties, your innovation may be delayed or derailed. If, despite your efforts, you cannot build the support of a value chain partner, you may need to redesign the business model so that the particular partner is not critical to its success.

Adoption chain risks are difficult to manage. They require truly understanding the needs and concerns of partners that seem far from the core innovation. Understanding these risks requires spending time in the ecosystem and envisioning what will be required. It means understanding the incentives—monetary and otherwise—required for the stakeholders to cooperate. It also means sharing the vision—and selling it—to people who have other things on their mind. The innovation must be big enough to create a sufficient surplus for this to work.

Apple has been masterful at managing co-innovation and value chain partner risks. Steve Jobs famously pressured Corning to produce Gorilla Glass to support its entry into the iPhone market, for example. At the time of the initial discussions, Gorilla Glass existed, but there were no plans to manufacture it. Steve Jobs insisted that Corning get into the business and he set the time frame to match the schedule for the release of the iTouch, which preceded the iPhone. Jobs was actively managing a co-innovation risk.

Jobs also worked relentlessly with music producers to garner their support for the iTunes store. At the time, music industry executives were very concerned about the cannibalization of their core CD business. Jobs had to create a revenue model and a vision of the future of music sales that enticed a critical mass of music rights holders to sell through iTunes. This process, which required vision, a clear understanding of the concerns of the value chain partners, and the ability to make the economic case for participation was critical to the success of first the iPod and then the iPhone.

The first step in identifying the full set of business model risks is simply to map them. Co-innovation risks are generally easy to identify, though assessing them may be quite difficult. To start, you simply need to identify all the elements of your offering and who is needed to provide them. A contractual arrangement alone, of course, does not guarantee success. It is important to take into consideration what it will take for your partner to succeed in helping you.

- Is the task they are undertaking routine for them, or does it require innovation?
- Is the customer domain one that is well-established for your partner, or does it involve new elements of risk?
- Can the partner scale up to deliver the necessary volumes at the price point desired?

The key question is this: What needs to be true for the partner to succeed?

Managing co-innovation risks means co-innovating, not simply delegating. You need to work closely with the innovation partner to provide information that may have been tacit, and both parties need to respond quickly as new issues arise. It is important that the whole team is comfortable raising issues, which can be difficult in a fixed-price vendor relationship. Establishing a working relationship at multiple levels between the partnering companies can be critical.

Managing adoption chain risks is more difficult. You need to start by understanding how the world looks today and how it will have to change once the new venture is launched. There may be many value chains that must be addressed for the product to succeed. Understanding who must do what in the new world means spending time in the ecosystem—walking through the steps in the process, from cradle to grave; having discussions with people who would need to do something differently; and seeking to elicit potential concerns when they seem to be both distant in time and contingent on success with other parts of the project.

It is helpful in assessing adoption chain risks to map relevant value chains and to capture specific areas where a change in operations might be needed. New requirements may be as simple as the availability of spare parts or as complex as process changes and modifications to IT systems that are outside of your control. In addition, the partners with whom you need to work may be fragmented, each with its own systems and ways of doing things.

It is important to ask, at each stage of the delivery process, who will need to know and do what. It can be difficult to surface some value chain issues without creating a set of specific scenarios—and trying to anticipate what might break them. Once a basic map is in place, it needs to be validated with those closest to the work. The process is inherently iterative.

Sometimes, management of the stakeholders for an entire ecosystem is overwhelming. In that case, it may be useful to envision what Adner calls a Minimum Viable Ecosystem (MVE). In an MVE, the offering might be confined to one customer segment, for example, or to a subset of the full suite of value chain partners, in order to simplify delivery.

To manage value chain risks, it is helpful to enumerate them and to assess them using a risk matrix, similar to those used in project execution. The matrix captures on one axis the willingness and ability of the partner to execute in a way that addresses the risk; the other axis captures the severity of the consequences to the program if it cannot.

Identifying and modeling risks may seem like a lot of effort, especially early in an innovation program. It pays three kinds of dividends, however. First, it increases the likelihood that you will bring a successful venture to market. With careful consideration of risks, it is far less likely that you will be surprised later, when much more is at stake. Second, it opens the door to finding ways of finessing some risks through re-design of your go-to-market model. Finally, it is more likely that you will include and account for *all* relevant costs.

In the second interview excerpt that accompanies this chapter, Ron Adner discusses the Wide Lens and the concept of the innovation ecosystem [Adner and Euchner, 2014]. His work highlights the fact that innovation today is increasingly complex and interdependent. It is unlikely that a company will control all of the resources necessary for success with a significant innovation. Adner introduces practical tools that innovators can use to identify members of an innovation's ecosystem, understand the motivations of those parties, and manage their alignment in order to increase the chances of success for your innovation.

## INNOVATION ECOSYSTEMS

## AN INTERVIEW WITH RON ADNER

When most organizations try to innovate, the primary focus of attention is on the innovation itself, including the commercial wrapper that makes it an actual business proposition. From there, attention moves to execution ... but implied within the proposition of many innovations is an additional set of factors and an additional set of actors that need to come together in order for the innovation's value to be realized.

That larger set of actors is the innovation ecosystem, and I believe that it is important to make that set of dependencies as explicit as possible as early as possible. When you think about the strategy for an innovation, you should be incorporating into that strategy all the dependencies and partnerships that are necessary for success and how you are going to align them to make the innovation work in the real world.

[There are two types of ecosystem risks to consider] Co-innovation risk concerns other innovations that need to be successful in order for your innovation to matter. You need to ask, does anyone else need to innovate to make my innovation successful? Those co-innovations can be product technologies, but they can be other kinds of changes required for success. Innovation is change, and it requires change among multiple parties.

[Adoption chain risk concerns] who else needs to buy in to enable adoption of my innovation? It is often the case that many parties need to agree to play. The critical issue when thinking about adoption chains is that the different parties will be approaching the choice of whether or not to participate based on their own concerns. They're going to think about their specific and idiosyncratic costs for participating and how those compare with their specific and idiosyncratic benefits of participating.

The mistake that too often is made is to look at innovation and see only how much better the world would be if it were implemented. Even if we know there's somebody in that adoption chain who's not going to be crazy about the innovation, the implicit assumption, the silent assumption, is that they'll come along because the overall concept makes so much sense. Time after time, we find that there are parties that *won't* come along, and it turns out that a little thing can hold back the whole innovation …

The question is, how do I create value *both within and for* the ecosystem? … The core tool that I developed to support this is the value blueprint. You start by depicting where you are and where your end customer is, and then you fill in all the parties necessary for success [with the new innovation.] … Go through the chain step by step and ask explicitly, "What else needs to happen in order for that party to move the innovation forward?" That process will help identify the co-innovators and the adoption chain partners …

The first thing that happens when you do a risk analysis of this broader system is that you see risk, and that's usually considered bad news. But the reason we do a risk analysis is precisely to see the risks so that we can act to mitigate them. It takes a lot of maturity to be calm in the face of these new moving pieces that we need to manage. The natural thing is to see the adoption chain risks and the co-innovation risks in addition to all your usual execution risks and ask, why am I even bothering to get out of bed? If you can do everything perfectly to create an innovation and the other guys can screw it up, why bother? …

[T]he philosophical difference between the Wide Lens approach and a more traditional approach to innovation [is that the] traditional path starts with a prototype to make sure we have a good idea, then we pilot it to make sure that we can really deliver everything required, then we move through different phases of expansion. The focus is about how to get to scale.

The alternative path, the Wide Lens path, starts with a prototype to make sure we have a good idea. But once we've established that, we seek to establish a minimum viable ecosystem, an MVE. The idea is to establish a commercial footprint that lets you manage a staged expansion, where you're adding partners over time, and with every additional partner you're enhancing the value proposition. At the end, you're at scale with a full value proposition, but your priority has been partners and value creation rather than racing to expand the single concept you had established at the pilot level.

It's very unlikely that you can line up all the partners for any meaningful innovation at the outset. If that's the goal, it's going to lead to paralysis. The principle of the minimum viable ecosystem tells us to take a step back and think about the bigger puzzle we want to assemble and then ask, what's the smallest subset of pieces that we can put together that allows us to create some kind of initial value? ...

## 4. Model the Risks to the Core Business

There is a variation of adoption chain risk that Adner touches on in his work. This is the risk associated with building support *within your own company* for innovation. To create a successful business model, you may need to leverage the assets of your company. To do so, you will require the support of the necessary functions to be successful. You may also need the support of senior business leaders who may be skeptical of the venture. It is well worth the time to create a stakeholder map to assess who in the company must support the venture and where they stand concerning it.

A useful practice for assessing internal risks is to explicitly model the effect of the new business on the core. Again, the model will be based on assumptions, but these can be reviewed, discussed, and tested. Such a model can shift the tone of internal reviews from a search for what might be hiding in the numbers to an assessment of how to reduce risks in order to move forward. Specific items modeled for Proactive Services were pull-through of tires from non-customers; increase in the share of a customer's wallet as a result of increased customer contact; reduced roadside assistance due to lower incidence of failure; increased capture of service performed as a result of the integration of the NewCo with the service network; and increased service revenues for installation of the telematics system. Just creating the list makes it clear that there are both opportunities and threats.

Finally, it can be useful to track (as best as you can) the metrics above. The Profit and Loss statement for the NewCo may not include these items, but an extended P&L can, and it makes clear the benefits of the new business to the larger company.

## 5. Reduce the Risks Using Business Experiments

As noted above, a business experiment (or what Eric Ries calls a Lean Learning Loop) starts with a hypothesis—which may be about almost anything important to your venture's success. The hypothesis needs to be clearly stated, in terms that are testable, in order to design an experiment to learn more about it. The experiment itself needs to be carefully designed so that it is effective, is executable, and can be undertaken quickly. The goal is to design a good-enough experiment that will reduce uncertainty quickly and cheaply.

Business experiments are in the real world, with real people in real contexts. Unlike science experiments, you can't really do a business experiment in the lab. Once the experiment is designed, you run it, which can sometimes be tricky. If you designed the experiment well and you conducted it honestly, you have either validated or invalidated one hypothesis. In the Lean Startup method, building a business is setting up a series of such hypotheses and knocking them down.

Designing a business experiment is both simple and difficult. It is simple in concept, but designing the experiment so that it can be conducted cheaply and provide a "good enough" answer quickly can be challenging. The first challenge is to define the hypothesis clearly. Nothing is more detrimental to good experiments than vaguely defined hypotheses. The goal is to isolate a particular important unknown and to state clearly what you think to be true.

The hypothesis may be related to sales: "We can sell the product through an email campaign."

It may be related to the product: "Our target segment will prefer a solution that is eco-friendly."

Or it may relate to costs: "We can set up a customer with our new product in less than 2 hours, on average."

To test a hypothesis, then, it needs to be stated in very specific terms. It needs to be designed to answer the question: "Is the hypothesis true?" The hypothesis to be tested might be made more specific with a concrete claim: "We can sell the product through an email campaign using our current customer list, and we will get a response rate of 5%." This is specific enough to test.

Executing a business experiment can also be complex. There is a tendency to want to do it perfectly—to design it as if it were part of a development activity rather than a lean experiment. It might be nice to integrate the email campaign with the customer relationship management system, for example, or to develop a great landing page for the product. The key, however, is to do something pragmatic to get a "good enough" answer quickly. This often means that everything is manual, the graphics are quick and dirty, and the prototype (if one exists) doesn't really function at all. All that is required for a good experiment is that it is close enough to reality to give a good indicator of truth.

The experiment may yield surprising results. Hypotheses in the realm of new venture creation are often wrong. You have to be willing to listen to the results of these experiments, whether they are positive or negative.

A well-designed business experiment has five attributes [Ganguly and Euchner, 2018]:

- It is focused on a key variable (not on many unknowns)
- It is specific and measurable
- It is appropriate to what needs to be learned (i.e., at the right level of fidelity)
- It is out in the world—with the market
- It is as fast and cheap as possible.

### BUSINESS DESIGN

### AN INTERVIEW WITH ADRIAN SLYWOTZKY

This discipline of business design is [getting to] the answer to ... six seemingly very simple questions, which turn out to be quite difficult to answer well.

The first question is, who is my customer and who is not my customer? There are a lot of problems if the answer is "anybody who pays." In business design, deciding who the customer is that we'll serve with our offer, and who we will not serve, is the point of departure. The first tough test is to assure that what we built really matches what this customer needs, wants, and will pay for.

The second question is, what is our unique value proposition? Why should the customer buy from us rather than from somebody else?

The third question addresses the profit model: how do we make money from this transaction or this relationship? The reason that this is a big question today and wasn't such a burning question 20 years ago is that 20 years ago the answer was simple: the player with the highest market share made the most money, so that's what companies aimed for ... [Market share is still] very important, but it's no longer the imperative. The key question now is, where and how will we be allowed to create profitability?...

The fourth in my list of questions and arguably the toughest is, what is our source of strategic control? That is to say, how do we protect the profitability that we create? It is important to protect profit not only from competitor imitation but also from growing customer power in the B2B world, or growing customer choice in the B2C world.

The fifth question is one of scope: what do we do ourselves and what do we procure from others or partner with others to do? ... The winning models from the early part of the 20th century into the third quarter of the century were integrated ... That has changed a lot, and everybody knows that.

But the question of what do we do ourselves and what we partner with others for is actually quite difficult for a couple of reasons. One is that we can't be brilliant at everything. We need to ask what are we planning to be world-best in. Second, not everything is really important. How do we make sure that we either undertake those important things ourselves or have a supplier or partner that does not get us into trouble? Finally, especially when you look at patterns of industry evolution, the important place in the value chain often changes with time ...

The last question to ask about business design is, how do we organize ourselves to make this happen? We need to think not just in terms of organizational structure but also in terms of the talent we develop or hire and the culture we create.

Answering these questions well is not easy. The overriding issue is that the answers match, that the model is coherent, so I don't wind up with a Jaguar engine and a Mercedes body and a BMW transmission and a Cadillac seat. The elements need to be mutually reinforcing; the model needs to work for both the customer and the economics ...

[When considering business designs, it is important] to develop alternatives. It is common for engineers to test two or three alternative versions of a product; companies should make it a practice to develop not just one good business design but three or four alternative designs for taking the same product or service to market. This exercise can be extremely powerful; there have been differences in the value created by alternative business designs in the same sector that are not 20 to 30%, but 5 to 10 *times* the value capture ... That simple question—What are three alternative business designs to take our new value to the customer, and which one will create the most value for us?—knocks people out of assuming the default business model is the best ...

The most efficient way to develop a model for your innovation is simply to leaf through [the two dozen models in *The Profit Zone*] and ask, are there three or four or five alternatives that are in the feasible set that we ought to explore?...

[Companies] used to be able to live in their industry's value chain, to butt heads in their value chain, to compete in their value chain. But this is breaking down. Now tech companies are competing against telco, against media, against consumer devices. They are expanding towards financial services, towards retail, towards education, towards health care. The thought process for successful companies is to focus on the hassle map of the customer, not on what value chain they are supposed to be part of. Their fundamental question is, how do I do a radically better job for the customer in fixing their hassle map? [M]ore and more competition will be across two, three, or four different value chains, not within a firm's original value chain ...

The complexity can kill you if you're trying to defend your original fort. The flip side is to seek simplification, which starts with the customer. If you can see the world through the eyes and emotions of the customer, you'll invariably see a mess. There's no industry that has been anywhere close to optimized. The winners are people who figure out how to not get anchored in the complexity but who look at the mess through the lens of the customer. Forty percent of that mess you might be able to solve yourself, but you may have to get parts from other places. Maybe that's a big difference: In the past, maybe 80 to 90% of the mess could be solved within a firm's value chain. In the new world, a company will probably be able to solve 20 to 30 to 40% by itself. If we're really looking at the problem from the customer's point of view, there will probably be a lot of pieces that we will have to license or hire in or acquire or work with the customer to solve.

Designing good business experiments is not easy. Three mistakes are common. First, the team can do an experiment that is just too vaguely defined. Often it is the hypothesis itself that is vague and, therefore, not testable. This can result in inadvertently testing several variables at once (and learning nothing). At other times, the measures of success are not defined ahead of time, so the results are subjective. These are not business experiments—even if they are out in the world—they are explorations.

On the other end of the spectrum, a team can make the experiment too complex or too high fidelity. The prototype used may be far closer to a product than is needed for the test, for example, or the team may seek to automate data collection instead of using people to do the grunt work. An over-designed prototype costs time and money, and it usually adds very little value. But many teams feel embarrassed to go to experiment with something simpler.

The best antidote to this tendency is for the team to envision three experiments to test the hypothesis and to challenge itself for the fastest, cheapest way forward. Sometimes it is helpful for outsiders to critique the experimental design and ask simplifying questions:

- Can we use a nonfunctioning prototype?
- Can people behind the scenes make the system seem real?
- Can we collect data on paper?
- What do you expect the output to look like?
- Where can we use proxy data to simplify the experiment?

The key is to challenge yourself to be simpler and faster—and then to challenge yourself again.

A third pitfall is to allow yourself to be constrained by perceptions of what you might be "allowed" to do.

- We can't talk to customers without going through sales
- We can't share an idea until we have filed the intellectual property
- We can't sell something that we don't have
- We can't show a customer a prototype that doesn't meet our brand standards.

On the one hand, these are real issues that must be navigated. Often, however, they are excuses for staying in the lab and bypassing good (and valuable) business experiments.

Business experiments can be designed to address uncertainties in all parts of the business. There are eight types of experiments that I have seen in multiple contexts (see Figure 7.2).

1. *Value creation experiments* are designed to understand the customer value your solution can create as well as what must be done by the customer to realize that value. The first step is to identify the categories of customer value, which can emerge from observation and customer interviews. The next step is to identify metrics for each category and to estimate ranges of expected changes as a result of the innovation. This data is helpful both in understanding the basic magnitudes involved and in highlighting what needs to be measured

**FIGURE 7.2**
Categories of business experiments

and what baseline data is required. Finally, the data are measured and the value is calculated.

2. *Willingness to pay experiments* focus on customer-perceived value and pricing. They usually are conducted through simulated transactions since people cannot usually state what they would do in the abstract. The New Earth Tire case discussed in Chapter 2 is one example of such an experiment.

3. *Channel effectiveness/efficiency experiments* test the reach, effectiveness, and cost of proposed channels for selling your offering. Channel effectiveness experiments, again, simulate real-world transactions. The experiments measure the number of targeted prospects reached and the number who purchase, usually as a function of promotional approach and price.

4. *Supply chain experiments* test the ability of the supply chain to provide the inputs required for the success of the business.

5. *Operational cost experiments* measure the costs of providing particular capabilities. Estimates are often good enough, but it is important at times to understand the underlying drivers of cost.

6. *Technology in use experiments* measure the delivery of value in the real world. There is often some erosion of value from the ideal when a new concept is introduced into a customer environment. This may be because anomalies in operations were not accounted for, because the technology requires more of a learning curve than expected, or because it is not as reliable as anticipated. Experiments in the real world with real customers can help to uncover these issues.

7. *Technology and human behavior* experiments. People often do not adapt to new technology as you might expect them to do. They may be intimidated by it; they may feel threatened by it; it might require adaptations to their work that are difficult to make. Learning these issues early is important. Once understood, they can often be designed for.

8. *Partner support level experiments.* Many new ventures require working with partners. Until the partnership is tested in some experiments, the level of support that will be provided in practice is unclear. Conducting targeted trials with key partners can help illuminate differences in priorities, clarify who is to do what, and assure that incentives are aligned.

Business experiments will never eliminate risk, so how long do you continue to invest in this learning? Different companies have different risk profiles. Some companies might go to market with high uncertainty (low predictability) about the profit that will be generated, as long as profit itself is likely in the long term: Time to market may be more important to them than the risk of a short-term loss. Others will want to invest more time and money in learning about key uncertainties and narrowing the ranges of key uncertainties before going to market.

## 6. Incubate the Business at Small Scale

The final step in bringing a new business model to market is to incubate it at a small scale in order to learn all those things that can only be learned in the market. Incubation requires setting up a functioning business, acquiring customers, setting prices, delivering the offering, managing expenses, and building a capable organization.

It is also during incubation that many of the issues with the core business are negotiated. Decisions about product development, IT support, contracts, liability clauses, etc., are resolved during this phase (see discussion of Graduated Engagement in Chapter 5).

In addition to demonstrating the profitability (or the potential for profitability) of the business, the team must also develop alternate plans for scaling the business during the incubation period. Inside a corporation, there are often multiple paths forward. The most obvious is to invest in the organic growth of the business. This can be done either to minimize losses or to maximize the success of the business (and absorb losses as the business invests in growth). The company might also decide to acquire capabilities or assets to accelerate the growth of the business. Finally, it might reorganize some of its current assets in order to structure the new venture for success. Each alternative needs to be considered prior to the decision to bring the business to scale.

The Business Model Pyramid provides a systematic way of developing and implementing a new business. It takes time, but it avoids the pitfalls of leaping into the unknown. Again, different companies will have different comfort levels with the amount of analysis required before proceeding through any level of the pyramid. It is important, however, to consider each step deliberately, in a manner consistent with your risk profile. Doing so greatly increases the chance of eventual success.

## KEY INSIGHTS

- Business model innovation is critical to capturing value from radical innovations
- Business model archetypes are the foundation for successful business model innovation
- Companies tend to lock onto their existing business models, even for very different value propositions
- It is useful to consider three or four business model alternatives before deciding how to go to market
- A new business model requires study before any attempt to implement it: Model the business, test the model, and benchmark companies in other industries that have successfully used it
- An assessment of ecosystem risks should be undertaken early
- It is helpful to think in terms of the Wide Lens: Execution risks, co-innovation risks, and value chain partner risks
- Some of the risks are initially hidden from view; you need to do fieldwork to really understand them
- Some of the risks are internal; an internal stakeholder map is useful in recognizing them
- Business experiments are the key tool for reducing risks
- Incubation assures that the new business model is truly understood before it is brought to scale.

# 8

## Organizing for Growth: The Separate-but-Connected Model

Deciding on the right organizational structure for a new business is a major challenge. As with all organizational decisions, it involves trade-offs. Tighter integration with the core business may enable the new venture to leverage corporate assets more easily. It can also reduce overhead, which can be a significant cost for a small entity. Finally, if a new business is integrated with the core business, it is less likely that the new business will be permitted to disrupt ongoing operations in the core.

Operating as a separate entity, on the other hand, allows the new venture to develop ways of doing things that are more appropriate to its status. It also protects the venture from political and budgetary challenges, which are deadly to many internal startups. Unfortunately, a separate entity inside a corporation often finds it difficult to leverage assets from the core business when it comes time to scale—and these assets may be at the very heart of competitive advantage.

According to Vijay Govindarajan, whose interview is included in this chapter, a new venture needs to do three things to operate successfully within the context of a larger business. It needs to *forget* some things, *borrow* others, and have the flexibility to *learn* still others.

*Forgetting* means walking away from deeply embedded assumptions that are not relevant to the new business. Many of the things to forget relate to the business model: Who the customers are, how they will be reached, what the nature of the offering is, and what level of support will be provided to customers. A new venture risks being shoehorned into the core business's existing business model, to the detriment of both. Any truly new venture must question the assumptions held deeply by

DOI: 10.4324/9780429433887-8

the core—figuring out which fit the new venture and which should be discarded.

A new venture inside a corporation also needs to *borrow* assets from the core business. The borrowed assets are the basis for competitive advantage for the new venture. Govindarajan estimates that a new venture inside a corporation should strive to have 40% of its required core competencies built on those of the core business. Leveraging these assets increases the chance that the new venture will be successful in the marketplace; it helps the venture to create a competitive advantage and overcome the disadvantages that derive from its corporate context.

Leveraging corporate assets is not easy. Borrowing assets from the core business creates immediate fears in the core: Fear that the new business will undermine the smooth functioning of the core; fear that it will succeed by cannibalizing the existing business; fear that the new business will bleed needed resources, both financial and human, from the core (which is already operating with demanding objectives). These fears must be managed if the assets are to be borrowed, which means that the manner in which these assets will be used and accounted for needs to be carefully designed and documented.

Of course, any new venture also needs to continue to *learn* what is necessary for success in its marketplace. Learning continues even once the business is in the market and being incubated. This in-market learning is an extension of the "with market" learning that was required to develop and test the offering and the business model. In order to do in-market learning, the venture needs a degree of independence. It must be able to make decisions quickly—about hiring, approaching customers, working with partners, or even competitors. The bureaucracy of the core business will suffocate the new venture if it is managed as part of the operating business.

## THE SEPARATE-BUT-CONNECTED ORGANIZATIONAL MODEL FOR NEW VENTURES

Govindarajan and Trimble propose that the tensions between a new venture and the core can best be balanced by setting up the new venture as an independent structure, with negotiated ties to the core business (see

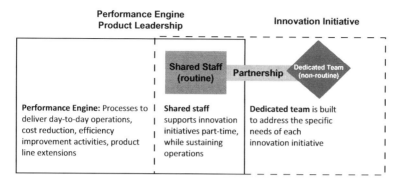

**FIGURE 8.1**

The Separate-but-Connected model adapted from Govindarajan and Trimble, 2010

Figure 8.1). The NewCo sits parallel to the existing business. While it has many of its own functions, it leverages the necessary capabilities of the core business through carefully negotiated agreements. The nature of these agreements varies by company and by venture.

Take as an example the Proactive Services business developed at Goodyear, discussed earlier in this text. The Proactive Services business monitors tires on commercial fleets in real time. It uses predictive analytics to alert customers of trucks that are at risk of a roadside tire failure due to poor tire maintenance. The concept relies on sensors, telematics, and cloud-based algorithms to create value. It must provide alerts for all tires, including those of competitors used by the fleet.

To succeed, the model needs to:

- "Forget" or relax the assumption that the company is a product company
- "Forget" the customer contact point within the customer to whom the offering will be sold, since the value proposition includes more than tires
- "Forget" or accept the fact that the offering may cannibalize roadside service and replacement tires.

It also needs to:

- "Borrow" access to customers
- "Borrow" access to the company's call center and service network
- "Borrow" the brand.

Of course, it also needs to continue to "learn" about costs, pricing, market segmentation, technology gaps, and other elements of the business model. This learning may crosscut what the core business has already learned and internalized.

Some of the assumptions about what to forget and what to borrow have obvious practical implications, but some are subtle. Although many ventures try to borrow the core company's sales force, for example, product salespeople can rarely sell a solution well. Trying to borrow this resource almost always fails. Similarly, the accounting system for a product business is very different than that of a services company, so services revenues will require both a specialized set of accounts and reconciliation with the corporate General Ledger system. This may not be obvious at first.

Proactive Services addressed these issues through a series of specific agreements, including, for example:

- *Sales*—A separate sales force for the new venture approached customers together with sales representatives from the core business; credit for any tire sales went to the representative of the core while credit for the services revenue went to the NewCo salesperson
- *Product*—Product required by the new business was purchased at "most favored nation" prices from the core business
- *Service*—Access to the service network was integrated into the new business; the cost of services was passed through to the services business P&L with no mark-up
- *Customers*—The new business updated customer records for the core business; the core maintained the master customer record; the NewCo maintained elements specific to its business.

Often, it is difficult for a business to accept the "Separate-but-Connected" model. Setting up a new business unit seems like a lot of overhead. The business argues that it currently manages a wide variety of projects; why should this one be so different?

Govindarajan's research with many companies shows that it is. Everything in a well-functioning and established business optimizes the dominant business model. Its distilled principles become the governing variables for important decisions about the new venture.

When there is a conflict, the dominant business model almost always wins. Without a separate organizational structure, the innovative venture almost always loses over time.

Sometimes, this dilemma plays out dramatically and publicly.

Kodak set up a separate digital photography business in 2001. By 2005, its EasyShare product was the leading digital camera. The core business was under financial pressure, however, and Kodak decided to merge the new unit into the core film business in an effort to reduce duplicate overheads. In short order, the digital business was starved for resources and shut down [Christensen, 2015].

Xerox famously invented the office of the future at the Xerox Palo Alto Research Center. The inventions included the first personal computer (the Alto), the bit-mapped computer display (including the desktop and icons), the mouse, the Ethernet, the laser printer, the first object-oriented computing language, and many other innovations. The company tried to bring the personal computer to market to large businesses through its direct sales force, but the costs of this channel were too high for personal computers. Both the target customer and the channel were mismatched with the product. Xerox profited from some of the innovations (like the Ethernet and the bit-mapped computer display) by incorporating them into its copier business, but it missed the potential of these innovations because they were trapped in its core business model.

Even Amazon had to separate the Marketplaces business from the core business in its early days. It found, when the Marketplaces business was just starting, that the core e-tail business resisted the idea of opening up its customer base to competitors—especially exposing, in some cases, competitor prices that were better than those of Amazon! [Rossman and Euchner, 2018].

## OVERCOMING RESISTANCE

In practice, setting up a separate business unit is politically fraught. The first argument is that it is not necessary. Running a new business as a separate unit will create duplicative overhead, make it harder to leverage resources like the sales force, and increase the risk of confusing customers with multiple offers.

One useful practice for overcoming this reluctance to form a separate operating unit is to engage decision-makers in a case study of companies that have faced the same dilemma. At Goodyear, when trying to make the organizational decision for Proactive Services, we worked with

Chris Trimble, Govindarajan's co-author, to review the dilemma faced by the *New York Times* as it considered the organizational structure for the new digital arm of the paper [Trimble, 2002]. The case was different enough from Goodyear's business to enable people to unlock from their organizational assumptions but, at the same time, highlighted a key issue that we faced. The leadership of the global commercial tire businesses participated actively in the discussion. At the end of the three-hour session, all participants recommended proceeding according to the Separate-but-Connected structure, at least for incubation. During that session, we also identified the key agreements that needed to be negotiated between the NewCo and the core business.

Another useful practice is to create a sequestered fund for the incubation of new businesses. This fund can be used for no other purposes; it is set aside so that it is available when a business is ready to go to market. The incubation fund takes away one of the major impediments to beginning incubation: The need to carve out the budget for doing so.

Incubation is for learning two key things: Whether the new business is profitable and what the alternative models are for bringing the business to scale. Once incubation is complete, the organizational decision must be considered again. The business-building strategy, for example, may be better executed by reorganizing some of the assets of the existing business as part of the NewCo. It may include an acquisition, which itself will have organizational implications. Or it may become clear that the NewCo can thrive within the structure of the core. I have seen all of these decisions succeed, as well as the decision to simply invest in the NewCo so that it can grow organically as an independent business. The right structure depends on circumstances. The key is to carefully reconsider the organizational question at key decision points and to do so with clear eyes.

## VIJAY GOVINDARAJAN ON *MAKING STRATEGIC INNOVATION WORK*

In *10 Rules for Strategic Innovators* and *The Other Side of Innovation*, Vijay Govindarajan and Chris Trimble discuss what it takes to innovate inside established companies [Govindarajan and Trimble, 2005, 2010]. They emphasize three concepts: *Forgetting* lessons from the past that may inhibit progress on a new venture; focusing on *learning* and clarifying key assumptions in the early stages of innovation; and consciously *borrowing* appropriate assets from the parent organization. These concepts may seem simple in principle, but they can be difficult to put into practice. The interview excerpt with Govindarajan included in this chapter discusses the practical implications of these ideas for innovators seeking to innovate within larger organizations [Govindarajan and Euchner, 2010].

## MAKING STRATEGIC INNOVATION WORK

### AN INTERVIEW WITH VIJAY GOVINDARAJAN

If you're serious about spending money to innovate a new business model, then get serious about the organizational question, because if you don't get that right, the opportunity is never going to materialize. When I'm asked for advice, I look into the CEO's eyes and say, "If you are really serious about innovation, you've got to make some tough, important decisions up front." ...

[Some of these decisions involve structure. In deciding how to structure for innovation,] the criteria to use is whether the innovation is breaking away from your current business model [or not]. You need to really think critically about the business model [implications] ...

A business model answers three questions: Who's your customer? What value is the customer seeking? And what is the process by which you're going to create that value? For your core business you have evolved an answer to these three questions.

If you are launching a new venture, and the innovation breaks away from your core business in its answer to any one of these three questions, then I'd say that you have to overcome [what I call] the *forgetting challenge* [emphasis added]. And one of the most effective ways to do that is to set up a separate venture ...

[The second challenge is] the *learning challenge* [emphasis added]. The reason you're experimenting is that you have a lot of unknowns. You want to get at least some firm understanding of what those unknowns are before you scale up and spend large amounts of resources. My golden rule is "spend a little, learn a lot." Because there are so many assumptions, you may be tempted to spend a lot. But in the experimental stage, what you're trying to do is to focus on your critical assumptions: those in the showstopper category and those in the category that requires you to fundamentally rethink your business strategy ...

[The *borrowing challenge* is one of deciding what you should] borrow from the host company to make a venture worth pursuing internally. [I do not suggest] moving into areas where you cannot leverage any of your critical assets. In that case, you would have no competitive advantage and the venture would be a pure startup. Pure startups, in Silicon Valley or somewhere else, have a big advantage in that they're not burdened by bureaucracy. They are nimble; they are fast; they can move. But the biggest advantage of a large company ... is its large resources, the established customer relationships, the core competencies. The only way the [large companies] of the world can win is by entering new spaces where they can leverage their capabilities.

[T]he projects with the most chance of success are what I would call adjacency-oriented new business model innovation. By adjacency, what I mean is adjacent to your core business. So, you are taking your current core competencies to a new customer. Or taking your core competencies and satisfying a need of your current customer better. Or taking your current competencies and pushing out into an adjacent space. Adjacency-oriented new business model innovation will utilize probably seventy-five percent of your core competencies.

The next step of innovation is what I call step-out. Step-out is not adjacency: you're stepping out of your core. [For Step-out adjacencies], if you have fifty percent of [the core competencies required] inside, I think that's a good step-out opportunity.

[Finding the balance between forgetting and borrowing can be difficult.] Using the framework [in *Ten Rules for Strategic Innovators*], you can increase your chances of getting it right on day one. It's better to get it right on day one, because if you overplay the forgetting challenge or underplay the borrowing challenge, you isolate and reduce the chances of success. The core business can sometimes squash such a venture.

On the other hand, if you keep the venture too close in order to maximize borrowing, then it may not have the ability to move to a new business model. The needs to forget and to borrow can pull you in different directions. It is possible to strike the right balance on day one, but keep an open mind because it may need to evolve. ...

[A key challenge companies have is how to] move from a large set of ideas to a few that you experiment with, and how [to] select the ones to scale up? I would say the following: most companies do it wrong because they only focus on the financial attractiveness of an idea. Financial attractiveness is fine, but I would ask another set of questions. For each of the ideas that you have, try to understand the assumptions you are making in order for this to be an attractive idea. Any kind of financial justification you can make for these ideas is all guesswork anyway, because there are so many unknowns. So instead, ask the question, what are the assumptions we are making for this idea to be a very profitable idea?

Take the assumptions that you are making and classify those assumptions into three groups. First are the showstopper assumptions; if these go wrong, the game is over. The second set of assumptions [are] those that require you to fundamentally rethink your strategy. And the third group of assumptions is ones you can tweak as you implement.

For ... NewCos, the operating review has to focus on the assumptions, because when you prepare your financial projections for a new venture, it's guesswork ... In the operating review, I want to focus on the ten assumptions that you identified up front, the critical assumptions. Use the operating review to tell me the experiments that you have done. Tell me what you have learned and how you are revising your plan as a result. Preparing a plan is important for clarifying the assumptions. Then you revise the plan based on what you have learned about those assumptions. That's what I'm going to judge NewCo on.

---

## KEY INSIGHTS

- Organization of a new business within an existing business is a critical issue
- The most successful practice is the formation of a separate NewCo with clear agreements with the core business about who does what, who will pay for what, and how joint work will be managed

- The organizational issue needs to be considered twice: First at incubation and then again at scale
- An incubation fund, sequestered for the sole purpose of incubating new businesses, is a key enabler in most companies.

# 9

## *Making the Bet to Win: Ambidextrous Leadership*

The biggest symptom of a failed innovation capability is a failure to make the bet to win. There are several reasons for this. The new venture may pose different kinds of risk than those in the core business, and executives may be uncomfortable making a big bet given the risk. Executives may fear that the new business will undermine the existing business and defer investment for that reason. Or executives may not feel prepared to defend the necessary investments to the investment community. These are all reasonable concerns.

But the failure to bet on new ventures often masks something more fundamental. In almost every corporation, there is a systematic avoidance of decisions that challenge the status quo.

Chris Argyris, a professor at Harvard Business School, has described this tendency in terms of models of organizational learning [Argyris, 1992].

Single loop learning is akin to the operation of a thermostat. If the temperature of the room is not at the set point of the thermostat, it closes a switch to turn on the heat or air conditioning. Single loop learning like this presents no issues for organizations. If something is amiss, according to established metrics of operations, people within the organization respond. A failure may implicate the performance of an individual or a department, but it does not challenge the organizational norms themselves.

Figure 9.1 depicts a schematic for single loop learning. The PDCA (Plan-Do-Check-Act) cycle is at the heart of the model. An important addition in Argyris' model is the box on the left, which represents the governing variables that guide decision-making. These may be thought of as the norms of the culture.

DOI: 10.4324/9780429433887-9

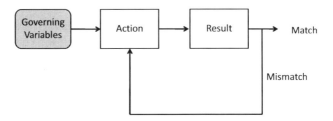

**FIGURE 9.1**
Single loop learning after Argyris

Most well-managed organizations excel at single loop learning. Its apotheosis is Six Sigma. In single loop learning, people observe and address any divergence from expected results.

Single loop learning can be a rigorous discipline, seeking root causes for deviations and addressing them rather than simply resolving the specific instance of a problem. Single loop learning has helped many companies significantly improve their operations. It is not, however, well-suited to most radical innovation.

Double loop learning, on the other hand, is learning about the system itself. There are circumstances under which any system ceases to function effectively. This failure often manifests itself in repeated attempts to solve a problem without success. An intervention may be designed to correct the problem, but the results of the intervention do not meet expectations. The cycle can go on ad infinitum, with repeated initiatives (which often, over time, are recycled).

Success with double loop learning requires challenging the governing variables of the system. To use the analogy above, it requires questioning the notion of the thermostat itself. Figure 9.2 is a schematic for double loop learning.

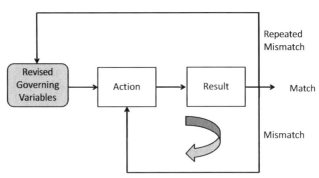

**FIGURE 9.2**
Double loop learning after Argyris

To be clear, a lot of innovation is possible without challenging the governing variables of the company. In fact, a useful categorization of innovation distinguishes between those types of innovation that operate within the bounds of the dominant business model (Type I innovation) and those that require changes to that model (Type II innovation). Figure 9.3 depicts these Basic Innovation Types.

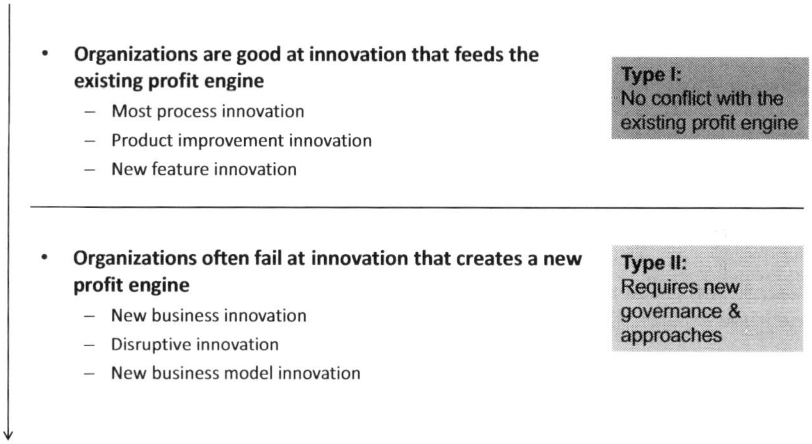

- **Organizations are good at innovation that feeds the existing profit engine**
  - Most process innovation
  - Product improvement innovation
  - New feature innovation

  **Type I:** No conflict with the existing profit engine

- **Organizations often fail at innovation that creates a new profit engine**
  - New business innovation
  - Disruptive innovation
  - New business model innovation

  **Type II:** Requires new governance & approaches

**FIGURE 9.3**
Two types of innovation

Type I innovation includes most process innovation. Process innovation fits well within the established governing variables of the business even if it involves radically new technologies. Also included in Type I innovation is the development of faster, better, or cheaper versions of your current offering. These offerings may integrate radically new technologies, but because the new product simply does a better job of delivering the same basic benefit to the customer, it does not require any change in operating assumptions about what works. Similarly, new product features may themselves be quite innovative and may create significant competitive advantage, but they do not challenge "the way things are done around here." Most innovation of this type succeeds most of the time in well-managed companies.

Type II innovation requires changes to some of the underlying assumptions about what works and does not work for the company. It usually requires violating one or more of the company's well-established governing variables. Type II innovation includes new business innovation, disruptive innovation, and some forms of "me, too" innovation. This type of innovation is generally very difficult inside existing corporations.

There are three governing variables that are active in most corporations and that can inhibit innovation. The company seeks always to act in accordance with these dicta:

1. To maintain focus
2. To do nothing that could damage the core business
3. To shepherd resources and direct them to the highest value return.

These operating rules make immense sense, all other things being equal. If your core markets are growing and if your competitive position is sustained or growing—in other words, if you have both the potential and the capacity for growth in your current business—then Type I innovation is sufficient for growth—and much lower risk than radical innovation. For Type I innovation, the existing governing variables will very likely support your innovation efforts.

If core markets are declining or your competitive position is eroding, on the other hand, it is very likely that some form of Type II innovation will be required. And such innovation will almost always challenge a core belief. Core beliefs are hard even to surface and challenge; Argyris makes the point that they are often so deeply embedded that they become undiscussable.

How does what Argyris calls an Organizational Defensive Routine (ODR) play out in practice? A goal is stated (and even embraced) that conflicts in some way with an (unstated) governing variable. People deny the conflict and suppress any discussion of it. This suppression assures that the conflict will not have to be addressed, and it acts to protect the core business from external challenges – even those that it might be vital to address.

Take an example related to innovation. Perhaps the espoused goal is to drive substantial growth outside the core business through new business innovation. The dysfunctional pattern starts with an inherent contradiction:

- *Explicit Goal*: We need to grow outside the core. We will invest in any new business ventures that make sense
- *Implicit Guiding Principle*: Protect (the current definition of) the core business at all costs.

These statements conflict with one another, but the conflict is not acknowledged. In fact, it is usually undiscussable. Why? It is part of many cultures to have a "can do" attitude; it is simply not acceptable to talk about apparently distant, hypothetical problems; one's focus should be on whatever it takes to move the project forward.

This seems to make sense, but it can prevent leaders from addressing an underlying issue. When a conflict between the new venture and existing norms arises—when the new business requires significant investment, for example—decision makers tend to default to the (implicit) guiding principles of the core business. The system acts to preserve resources for the core. In these battles, the governing variables of the dominant business almost always win, which means that the innovative venture almost always loses.

It is difficult work to both operate with excellence in the current business and challenge its most established norms. What is required is what Michael Tushman terms "ambidextrous leadership" [O'Reilly and Tushman, 2004]. Ambidextrous leaders develop the capacity both to *exploit* the current business and to *explore* new businesses, in spite of the fact that the skills and mindset required for these roles are so different. Figure 9.4 compares the two.

A key to ambidextrous leadership is the ability to discuss conflicts that are created when a company tries to innovate. This means getting past the organizational defensive routines to understand the differing cultural norms required for success with the two types of innovation [Argyris, 1992].

Tushman has identified two types of ambidextrous leadership. The first is *structural ambidexterity*. In structural ambidexterity, the new venture is managed completely separately from the core business, often in a different location. The new venture has its own functions and develops its own culture and set of governing variables. The executive leading the NewCo likely has attributes of an "explore" mindset. The new business

| | Exploitative Business | Exploratory Business |
|---|---|---|
| **Strategic intent** | Cost, Profit | Growth, Innovation |
| **Critical tasks** | Efficiency<br>Incremental innovation | Adaptability<br>New products |
| **Competencies** | Operational | Entrepreneurial |
| **Structure** | Formal | Adaptive, Loose |
| **Controls** | Margins, Productivity | Milestones, Growth |
| **Culture** | Low risk<br>Quality<br>Customer focus | Risk taking<br>Speed<br>Experimentation |
| **Leadership role** | Top down | Visionary |

**FIGURE 9.4**
Ambidextrous leadership after O'Reilly and Tushman

comes together with the established business only at the level of the CEO. This type of ambidextrous leadership works if the CEO has the skills to hold the tension himself or herself and to make difficult decisions about resource allocation in the face of resistance from other key executives.

The second type of ambidextrous leadership is team-centric ambidexterity. It depends on developing, over time, a cadre of leaders who can both exploit the existing business and explore new businesses. These skills must be buttressed by a set of leadership practices and incentives that encourage the right behaviors. According to Tushman, team-centric ambidextrous leadership is more difficult to create and sustain. It will be increasingly important in the future, however, as the half-life of business models becomes shorter and shorter.

## MICHAEL TUSHMAN ON *AMBIDEXTROUS LEADERSHIP*

Michael Tushman has studied executive leadership teams and what makes some more effective than others in driving innovation. He has found ambidextrous leadership at the core of successful companies. A starting point for ambidextrous leadership is simply to acknowledge the differences between managing the core business and managing an emerging business. Unfortunately, this is difficult in practice. In the interview excerpt that accompanies this chapter, Tushman discusses what works, why, and what it takes to create an ambidextrous organization—one that can nurture and invest in new growth businesses [Tushman and Euchner, 2015].

### THE CHALLENGES OF AMBIDEXTROUS LEADERSHIP
### MICHAEL TUSHMAN ON AMBIDEXTROUS LEADERSHIP

#### AN INTERVIEW WITH MICHAEL TUSHMAN

The fundamental idea [of ambidextrous leadership]—which has been around in the innovation field for a while—is that companies need to develop dynamic capabilities at the business unit level and at the corporate level to play two games at once. The first is to *exploit* the existing strategy and the second is to *explore* an uncertain future.

Firms that do both well survive over time; firms that get stuck in either exploit or explore don't do well ...

Our solution to the problem ... is structural ambidexterity: companies need to separate the exploit franchise from the explore franchise. They need to be physically separate, culturally separate, with separate finance functions, because they have completely different architectures for competencies and culture.

The goal for the exploit crowd is to get better and better, to meet the numbers; the goal for the explore crowd is to figure out the future before your competitors do. You do that through making a bunch of mistakes, by failing forward, learning by doing, employing Lean Startups to very rapidly prototype and learn from your mistakes so that you discover the future before others do. Structural ambidexterity is keeping the past separate from the future.

There are three hallmarks of structural ambidexterity: high differentiation, targeted integration where there's leverage, and really strong senior team integration ...

In order for ambidexterity to work, you need to take advantage of synergies across the two worlds. Probably the biggest issue companies face is developing senior teams that can handle paradox, that can handle living in two different worlds—the world of the future and the world of the past—and can share resources and co-create both these worlds simultaneously ...

Not everyone needs to live in both worlds; not everyone needs to make the trade-offs between explore and exploit. Most of the organization is exploiting, and some significant part of the organization—located someplace else—is exploring. The only place that this tension is held is with the ambidextrous leadership team.

I have seen different structures for this. Both the hub-and-spoke or leader-centric and the team structure can work ... I think that the more effective and more resilient way of managing ambidexterity is having senior teams that own the tension, and developing the capability in those teams to make the decisions that trade off assets between the explore and exploit businesses ...

My experience with the CEOs of established companies is that they systematically underprioritize the importance of exploration and systematically overprioritize exploitation. That's what the market wants; that's what your shareholders want; that's the way senior leaders are often coded. A company may be viewed by Wall Street as a stock that is stable and not high tech, yet sometimes a company like that can get destabilized fast ...

What makes ... ambidexterity ... work is a senior team that is able to accommodate completely different cultures for the exploit and explore businesses. The exploit culture is a culture of not making any mistakes; it's a culture of discipline; it's a culture of process. The explore culture needs to be very different—[it needs to be] one of risky experimentation, one where people are willing to make a bunch of mistakes, to learn quickly from them, and to make big changes ...

I have found the concept of the opportunity gap to be useful [in helping CEOs to grasp the importance of the explore parts of their jobs]. Opportunity gaps are always rooted in a proactive strategic shift. [They enable firms to] move before they have to ... It helps leaders see that you can't get to the future just by exploiting, that that's a recipe for disaster. The hard problem is figuring out the right pace, rate, and intensity of exploration ....

[P]robably the hardest challenge for executives in this ambidexterity game [is] driving change in really successful organizations that get tied up in the present. If they are not careful, all of a sudden someone may come in from left field and destabilize the business model pretty fast ...

Great ambidextrous teams have to be heterogeneous. The challenge is that, in general, heterogeneous teams don't work because they have to overcome significant differences in the approaches of the team members. What you need are heterogeneous teams that have both a leader and a team process that let you get the team differences out and adjudicate them.

You may have a homogenous team doing the exploit and a homogenous team doing the explore, but ambidextrous teams that are living in these contradictory worlds need to be heterogeneous. As I noted earlier, there is a hub-and-spoke structure that is leader-centric and is not really team-y at all. The CEO stands in the middle and holds the paradox personally. That's really hard; it's very brittle. It's difficult to sustain that tension in one person ...

[V]ision is important in making [the combination of exploit and explore] happen: Here's what we're doing and, more importantly, here's why we're doing it. If there is passion around an overarching purpose, it frees senior teams from a lot of implicit assumptions ...

[O]ne of the things that makes a big impact in actually getting this stuff done ... is helping people deal with the implications of the change for their own personal identities ... The point is that the change initiative can't stop with defining a broader identity for the firm. The professional identity of the people in the organization is also important ...

## KEY INSIGHTS

- Innovation often fails because of an inability to "bet to win" once a new business has been validated
- This failure can be traced to the difficulty executives can have exploring new businesses while focused on exploiting the existing business
- New businesses require executives to make decisions with different mindsets than those that are socialized through the governing variables of the core business
- Ambidextrous leadership can help to overcome the challenge
- Structural ambidexterity is more likely to succeed (today) than team-based ambidexterity.

# 10

## Yes … And: Making Lean Startup Work in Large Organizations

Both startups and new ventures inside corporations must manage similar conditions of extreme uncertainty: Will the market for the new offering develop? How quickly? Can the product be delivered at an attractive cost? Will people be willing to pay for it? Will the new technology work? What new competitors might disrupt the business? These are *market* uncertainties, and they are the province of entrepreneurs. The Lean Startup methodology is designed to reduce these risks systematically, quickly, and at a low cost.

A venture inside a corporation also deals with internal risks that startups do not face. These risks come in three general categories: Personal risks, risks to the performance engine, and risks to the corporation itself.

- *Personal risks* are the career risks taken by innovators who associate themselves with, champion, or spend time on a venture that may not succeed—one that may even make enemies in the core business. Most corporate environments are far less tolerant of a good failure than a robust startup ecosystem is, whatever the declarations of executives to the contrary. For an individual, the career risk also includes the opportunity cost of spending time off the mainstream career path
- *Risks to the performance engine* are risks that core functions confront in their support of innovation. These functions include sales, intellectual property law, liability law, procurement, IT, engineering, and contracts. Support of the new venture may distract people in

DOI: 10.4324/9780429433887-10

these functions from their core objectives. It may also result in errors as the functions struggle to deal with issues very different from those they confront in their support of the core business

- *Risks to the corporation* operate at a higher level. They are the (perceived) risks that the new venture will cannibalize the existing business and sap resources, both financial and human, that the core business needs. There is also a potential risk that the new venture will drag the business away from its successful core.

To succeed, internal ventures must complement the practices of the Lean Startup approach with others peculiar to the corporate context. The differences between the startup context and the corporate context need to be managed in addition to and in coordination with the Lean Startup method [Euchner, 2019].

## COMPLEMENTARY PRACTICES FOR LEAN STARTUP IN LARGE ORGANIZATIONS

Lean Startup practices solve a major problem (taking the risks out of a new venture), but they do so at a cost. Implementing these practices within a corporate setting can provoke corporate antibodies. The pressures of organizational life can cause people to act in a way that inhibits the progress of the innovation team. These natural tendencies need to be identified and managed.

One useful way to approach this dilemma is to look at the sources of resistance through the lens of the Lean Startup practices themselves. Although the relationship between Lean Startup approaches and internal resistance is not one-to-one, each practice does induce specific kinds of resistance and internal challenges (Table 10.1). The first three practices of the Lean Startup, which relate to the daily work of the innovation team, create concerns about the day-to-day operations of the business. The next three deal with a more fundamental issue—the compatibility of the venture with its host corporation. This book explored six practices that can help companies to resolve the dilemma. These complementary practices are summarized below.

Table 10.1 summarizes the relationship between Lean Startup principles and the complementary practices.

**TABLE 10.1**

Tools for Resolving Dilemmas Presented by Lean Startup Practices

| Lean Startups must … | But … | So internal ventures must also … | Through additional practices, such as … |
|---|---|---|---|
| Iterate using Lean Learning Loops | Corporations hate processes that look unmanaged and chaotic | Demonstrate disciplined innovation | An Innovation Stage-Gate |
| Develop an MVP to get market feedback quickly | Core functions resist provisional concepts (and tend to delay or stop experimentation) | Find a way to work with core functions to make things happen | Graduated Engagement |
| Create a Value Hypothesis (achieve product-market fit) | An internal venture must leverage corporate assets to create a competitive advantage | Develop a growth agenda that is accepted by corporate leaders | Asset-Based Opportunity Spaces |
| Develop a viable business model (the Business Hypothesis) | New business models are risky and can threaten the core business | Manage the risks to the dominant business model | The Business Model Innovation Pyramid |
| Create a Growth Hypothesis to build an organization that can scale | Corporate cultures often smother a new venture | Organize to leverage corporate assets and protect the venture | The Separate-but-Connected model for incubation |
| Bet to win | Executives inside corporations are often focused on execution, not innovation | Develop structures and skills that enable double loop learning | Ambidextrous leadership |

*Adapted from Euchner, "Yes … And: Making Lean Startup Work in Large Organizations."*

## 1. Innovation Stage-Gates: *Reconciling Lean Learning Loops with the Need to Demonstrate Discipline*

The Lean Startup methodology is somewhat chaotic. It works, when it works well, because the chaos is managed through a learning agenda. Over the course of a monthly sprint, many things can change: The feature set of an MVP, the target customer, the channel to market, the revenue model. To executives used to evaluating whether or not a project is on plan and on budget, this constant change can be unsettling, even with frequent reviews and good documentation of the decisions made. Executive leadership teams often want a more linear assessment of progress.

The use of an Innovation Stage-Gate process with clear intermediate deliverables and a reasonable estimate of time frames for creating them can provide the necessary framework (see Chapter 4). In an Innovation Stage-Gate system, the process within the stages is agile, dynamic, and a bit chaotic; at the level of the gate deliverable, however, it is more defined and more predictable.

Introducing an Innovation Stage-Gate process requires separating in time some of the activities that might be undertaken simultaneously in the Lean Startup approach [Ganguly and Euchner, 2018]. Customer insight and the development of the customer value proposition can be usefully separated from creation of the business model, for example. Similarly, business model development can be separated from in-market incubation of the concept, reducing the risks of entering the market. Finally, the decision to scale the venture can be separated from the decision to incubate it. In essence, an Innovation Stage-Gate is simply the unraveling of the hypotheses at the vertices of the Lean Startup triangle.

A stage-and-gate process may strike some as antithetical to the Lean Startup approach—and even to innovation itself. It is, however, a critical element in matching the Lean Startup to other business processes in large organizations. The stage-and-gate structure provides a clear sense of progress, clear points at which investment decisions can be made, and a space where executives can learn, over time, about a new market and its risks and promise.

## 2. Graduated Engagement: *Developing MVPs in the Context of the Performance Engine*

Every established company has what Vijay Govindarajan and Chris Trimble call the "performance engine." [Govindarajan and Trimble,

2010]—the collection of functions, processes, and resources that have been optimized over time to support the profitability of the core business. The people who manage the performance engine have objectives, internal client expectations, and methods of operating that can be disrupted by an innovation team—especially one focused on breakthrough innovation. Nevertheless, the internal venture needs to leverage the skills, resources, and *imprimatur* of the internal functions.

How can an organization resolve this paradox and create an environment where the performance engine and the new venture can co-exist— and even support one another? Some companies create an entirely independent innovation entity, with its own HR, IT, procurement, legal, and engineering functions. This approach is expensive and, in many cases, impractical. Others attempt to use the existing functions, together with pressure from the top, to get things done. This works well until it wears thin, and then it tends to collapse.

There is a third way, one that engages the performance engine throughout the innovation process in a transparent but graduated way. In essence, core functions provide basic support during the exploratory parts of the process and only become more engaged as the concept advances. Decision rights are explicitly negotiated for each stage in the Innovation Stage-Gate process. The various functions provide the support needed, using budgeted funds allocated for that purpose. The innovation function assumes the risk of doing things differently and more quickly; it is the responsibility of the functions simply to highlight issues they anticipate and to make the risks explicit. When the venture moves into incubation, the functions become more active in assuring (appropriate) compliance with established practices (see Chapter 5).

Graduated engagement assures that existing standards and ways of working, which often seem very constraining for those doing something new, will not slow down the innovation team as the business is being developed. It also assures that the venture will comply with corporate standards once it is launched. Implementing this kind of ramped engagement takes time, planning, open communication, and compromise, but it enables an internal venture to move quickly and to do so in a way that still leverages corporate knowledge and resources—one of the primary advantages corporate ventures have over startups.

## 3. Opportunity Spaces: *The Value Hypothesis and the Need to Create Strategic Alignment*

An ongoing corporation has strategies, whether they are explicitly stated or implicitly enacted. Any new venture must align with these strategies or with an explicitly espoused growth strategy. If executives cannot see the connection between a new venture and a larger corporate objective; if they do not see the value in spending the time necessary to understand a new domain in sufficient depth to make investment decisions with confidence; if the new venture is seen as diverting resources from the existing corporate strategy rather than moving it forward, then investment will not flow.

One way of achieving this alignment is by creating sanctioned opportunity spaces. Assets of the corporation—including the customer base, the brand, the service network, and core technologies—provide a basis for future competitive advantage. They can often be combined with market opportunities in a way that provides a unique advantage.

Shaping the opportunity space within which a corporation will play and making it explicit is difficult work. It requires thinking through alternative spaces, understanding their potential for the company, and being realistic about corporate assets. This is not something that senior leaders can delegate. But once the opportunity space is sanctioned, it reduces the concern that the innovation initiative is going off in irrelevant or even destructive directions (see Chapter 6). Of course, startups must also define their opportunity spaces, but they do not have to align them with an external strategy, as internal ventures must.

## 4. The Business Model Pyramid: *The Business Model Hypothesis and the Need to Manage Internal Risks*

A business model is a configuration of resources, assets, and processes designed to deliver a customer value proposition profitably. A good business model creates differentiation in the marketplace and has economic leverage—it gets stronger with scale. Over time, a company's business operations become optimized, and when they reach this stage, the business model is resistant to change. Introducing a new business model appears to be both costly and risky. It means going back to square one and learning anew how to drive profitability.

Business models that leverage assets and are compatible with a corporation's strategy can be systematically developed (see Chapter 7). The Business Model Pyramid is a useful tool for doing so. It moves systematically from the value proposition to incubation. It starts by considering multiple business model options and identifying the risks of each. A key element is understanding in a quantitative way any risks to the core business (in addition to market and execution risks). Use of the Business Model Pyramid is helpful in managing internal resistance by making the risks (as well as the opportunity) explicit, and by creating clarity about the impact of the new venture on the core business.

## 5. Organizing for Growth: *The Growth Hypothesis and the Separate-but-Connected Organizational Model*

Organizational issues do not loom large when a venture inside a large company is small. Everyone involved does whatever is necessary for success. Resources are begged, borrowed, stolen, and cajoled into being. (This is true for startups, as well, although the sources of resources are different.) As the venture matures, both startups and internal ventures need to manage a new set of challenges. In both cases, for example, the leadership may need to change as the venture enters the growth stage. The team must often be reshaped to take full advantage of the opportunity the venture has created.

An internal venture has an additional set of issues to address. When it was small, it could fly under the radar. As long as it was able to muster the resources it needed and the permissions required to operate, it was not challenged. But growth changes this balance. Suddenly, the new venture challenges the *status quo* in ways that were not visible when it was small. It may attract scarce budget, draw on scarce internal talent, and demand managerial time from the core business. The core often fights back (if it feels it has the political permission to do so). Moving the venture from incubation to scale must therefore be done carefully, especially if the business intends to leverage the assets of the core business.

Internal ventures fail when the balance is poor—when integration is too tight to accommodate differences in business models or when the separation is so complete that the parent venture confers no competitive advantage. Too tight an integration can mean that the new business is force-fit into the existing business model, with the functions, routines, and policies of the core grafted onto the new venture—whether they support it or not. Too tight an integration can also lead to investment that is governed by normal corporate allocation processes, not by the opportunity the venture presents.

Full separation of the new venture and the core business brings other risks. The primary danger of full separation is that the assets of the core will not be available to help the venture create a competitive advantage. Without these advantages, the new venture might as well be a startup.

The Separate-but-Connected model for achieving the needed balance between the core business and the new venture calls for structural separation together with explicit, negotiated relationships between the new venture and the core business functions (see Chapter 8). Applying this model requires open discussion that is often difficult in a corporate context, as the organizational issue inevitably impinges on issues of power and budgets. It is helpful—perhaps essential—to sequester funds to incubate the business so that the questions concerning organization are not fraught with budget issues.

## 6. Making the Bet to Win: *Ambidextrous Leadership*

There is another risk that must be balanced differently inside a corporation—the risk associated with the "bet to win." Once a venture has been brought to the point where it has proven to be attractive to customers, profitable, and scalable, a venture capitalist will often go all-in to win in the marketplace. The corporate investor, confronted with alternate investment paths, will often choose the path that minimizes the downside risk rather than the one that maximizes the venture's potential. This is understandable. It can be hard for a public company to explain to Wall Street a dip in earnings due to significant investment in a new and very different business. Getting to the point where the resource allocations match the opportunity requires double loop learning and ambidextrous leadership, the subject of Chapter 9.

Ambidextrous leadership skills are built up over time. Executives may be emboldened and invest more aggressively in a new venture if the corporation has implemented some of the practices recommended in this book to help the leadership team understand the opportunity and its risks.

## CONCLUSION

The Lean Startup method has been demonstrated to work well, especially for startups and software companies. Successfully applying the method within established companies—especially industrial companies—has been problematic. This is due, in part, to the reaction of the organization to the elements of the Lean Startup method itself.

There is a set of practices that have proven successful in overcoming resistance and launching new ventures within established companies. These practices—or similar practices that address the same underlying issues—need to be implemented to complement the deployment of Lean Startup. Breakthrough innovation is a *Yes ... And* proposition. While Lean Startup practices are useful for creating new businesses under conditions of extreme uncertainty, the complementary practices address the threats that Lean Startup creates in established companies. Both are necessary for success.

# References

Adner, R. 2013. *The Wide Lens: What Successful Innovators See That Others Miss.* New York: Penguin Group.

Adner, R. and Euchner, J. 2014. Innovation Ecosystems. Conversations. *Research-Technology Management* 57(6): 10–14.

Argyris, C. 1992. *On Organizational Learning.* Oxford, UK: Blankwell Publishers Ltd.

Blank, S. 2012. Making a Dent in the Universe – Results from the NSF I-Corps. Blog post, June 11, 2012. Steveblank.com.

Blank, S. 2013. *The Four Steps to the Epiphany: Successful Strategies for Products That Win.* K&S Ranch.

Blank, S. 2021. Private communication.

Blank, S. and Euchner, J. 2018. The Genesis and Future of Lean Startup: An Interview with Steve Blank. Conversations. *Research-Technology Management* 61(5): 15–21.

Blank, S. and Euchner, J. 2021. Lean Startup and Corporate Innovation. Conversations. *Research-Technology Management* 64(5): 11–17.

Christensen, C. and Euchner, J. 2011. Managing Disruption: An Interview with Clayton Christensen. Conversations (reprint). *Research-Technology Management* 63(3): 49–54.

Christensen, C. and Raynor, M. 2003. *The Innovator's Solution: Creating and Sustaining Successful Growth.* Cambridge, MA: Harvard Business School Publishing.

Cooper, R., Edgett, S. and Kleinschmidt, E. 2002. Optimizing the Stage-Gate Process – What best practice companies do – I. *Research-Technology Management* 45(5): 21–27.

Cooper, R., Edgett, S. and Kleinschmidt, E. 2002. Optimizing the Stage-Gate Process – What best practice companies do – II. *Research-Technology Management* 45(6): 43–49.

Euchner, J. 2019. Yes…And: Making Lean Startup Work in Large Organizations. *Research-Technology Management* 62(6): 36–43.

Euchner, J. and Ganguly, A. 2014. Business Model Innovation in Practice. *Research-Technology Management* 57(6): 33–39.

Ganguly, A. and Euchner, J. 2018. Conducting Business Experiments: Validating New Business Models. *Research-Technology Management* 61(2): 27–36.

Gassmann, O., Frankenberger, K. and Choudhury, M. *The Business Model Navigator: The strategies behind the Most Successful Companies.* Harlow, England: Pearson.

Goldstein, V. and Euchner, J. 2017. Transformation for Growth at GE. Conversations. *Research-Technology Management* 60(6): 14–19.

Govindarajan, V. and Euchner, J. 2010. Making Strategic Innovation Work: An Interview with Vijay Govindarajan. Conversations. *Research-Technology Management* 53(5): 15–20.

Govindarajan, V. and Trimble, C. 2005. *10 Rules for Strategic Innovators: From Idea to Execution.* Boston, MA: Harvard Business Review Press.

Govindarajan, V. and Trimble, C. 2010. *The Other Side of Innovation: Solving the Execution Challenges.* Boston, MA: Harvard Business Review Press.

Kelley, T. 2002. *The Art of Innovation*. London: Profile Books Ltd.

Kelley, T. 2005. *The Ten Faces of Innovation*. New York: Currency/Doubleday.

Koen, P., Golm, N. and Euchner, J. 2014. IRI Research on Research: Lean Startup in Large Organizations. Internal discussions. Unpublished.

Lanning, M. 1998. *Delivering Profitable Value: A Revolutionary Framework to Accelerate Growth, Generate Wealth, and Rediscover the Heart of Business*. New York, NY: Basic Books.

Moore, G. 1991. *Crossing the Chasm*. New York: Harper Collins.

O'Connor, G. and Euchner, J. 2017. The People Side of Breakthrough Innovation: An Interview with Gina O'Connor. Conversations. *Research-Technology Management* 60(4): 12–18.

O'Reilly, C. and Tushman, M. 2004. The Ambidextrous Organization. *Harvard Business Review*. April 2004.

Olson, D. 2015. *The Lean Product Playbook: How to Innovate with Minimum Viable Products and Rapid Customer Feedback*. Hoboken, NJ: John Wiley & Sons.

Osterwalder, A. and Euchner, J. 2019. Business Model Innovation: An Interview with Alex Osterwalder. Conversations. *Research-Technology Management* 62(4): 12–17.

Osterwalder, A. and Pigneur, Y. 2010. *Business Model Generation*. New Jersey: Wiley.

Ries, E. 2011. *The Lean Startup: How Today's Entrepreneurs Use Continuous Innovation to Create Radically Successful Business*. New York: Crown Publishing.

Ries, E. 2017. *The Startup Way: How Modern Companies Use Entrepreneurial Management to Transform Culture and Drive Long-Term Growth*. New York: Crown Publishing.

Ries, E. and Euchner, J. 2013. What Large Companies Can Learn from Startups: An Interview with Eric Ries. Conversations. *Research-Technology Management* 56(4): 12–16.

Ritti, R. and Funkhouser, G. 1977. *The Ropes to Skipo and the Ropes to Know*. Columbus, Ohio: Grid, Inc.

Rossman, J. and Euchner, J. 2018. Innovation the Amazon Way. Conversations. *Research-Technology Management* 61(1): 13–22.

Slywotzky, A. 2002. *The Art of Profitability*. New York: Warner Books.

Slywotzky, A. and Euchner, J. 2015. Business Design. Conversations. *Research-Technology Management* 58(1): 12–18.

Slywotzky, A. and Morrison, D. 2000. *How Digital Is Your Business?* New York: Crown Business.

Slywotzky, A. and Morrison, D. 2002. *The Profit Zone: How Strategic Business Design Will Lead You to Tomorrow's Profits*. New York: Three Rivers Press.

Stone, B., Larkin, P., et al. 2013. *The Everything Store*. New York: Little, Brown & Company.

Trimble, C. 2002. New York Times Digital (A, B, C). Dartmouth, Tuck School Business Case.

Tushman, M. and Euchner, J. 2015. The Challenges of Ambidextrous Leadership. Conversations. *Research-Technology Management* 58(3): 16–20.

# Index